I0118903

A TEENAGER'S COMPASS TO LIFE

Proverbs, Sayings, Quotes, and Jokes

To Help Point The Way

Compiled by Izzi Tooinsky

The King of Hotdogastan

A Teenager's Compass to Life

Proverbs, Saying, Quotes, and Jokes to Help Point The Way

The text in this book has been compiled by Izzi Tooinsky and has been cited for authorship. The illustrations, including cover art, are either public domain or have been created by Izzi Tooinsky.

First edition published November 8, 2024.
© 2024 Izzi Tooinsky and Royall, LLC. All rights reserved.
Published by Cabanga, an imprint of the Royall company
128 Race St., Grass Valley, CA 95945.   +1 (808) 301-0535
In association with the Hotdogastan Jugglers Guild.

ISBN 979-8-9914547-2-8 Paperback

For copyright permissions contact Cabanga books
or visit www.izzitooinsky.com for more information.

The Greatest Lesson

"The greatest thing you'll ever learn,

is just to love

and be loved in return."

Eden Ahbez

Proverbs in Conversation

"Proverbs in conversation are torches in darkness."

Venezuelan Proverb

Inside Me

"Inside of me, there are two Wolves.

One is mean and selfish, and the other is good and understanding.

They fight each other all the time. When asked which one will win, I answer,

The one I feed the most."

Sitting Bull

Dedication

For Silas and Brianne, and all the other teens who continue to bring so much joy, surprise, insight, and love into my life.

May this book help to guide you all on your own, amazing, individual journeys.

Acknowledgments

I would first like to thank my mom, the Matriarch of Hotdogastan, for her commitment to healing and recovery in our family and beyond.

I would like to thank my wife Janice, for her obvious deep heart, for being patient with me, and for believing in the value of this book.

I would like to thank my cousin Paulette, for being my friend and companion through all these wonderful and tumultuous decades.

A big thank you to my friend and editor Martin Webb. May other authors be graced by his skill, clarity and humor.

Table of Contents

Short History of
A Teenager's Compass to Life

No one knows when or where this book was first written. It has been updated, translated, and revised thousands of times throughout the centuries. Legend says that the first versions were handwritten by teens on the inside of birch bark. In later years, the entire book was written on sheepskin parchment, and at some point, it was copied onto rice paper scrolls and carried far and wide across the planet.

In 1590, A *Teenager's Compass to Life* was first printed and bound with leather by the legendary Russian adventurer and printer Ivan Goofinoff. One hundred years later, a single, tattered copy was carried to Hotdogastan where it was immediately recognized as a treasure by the indigenous people. It has become such an important part of the nation that, still to this day, an image of *A Teenager's Compass to Life* can be seen on the bottom left corner of the Hotdogastan national flag.

A Little About Hotdogastan

Hotdogastan is a very ancient, extremely small country. It's not far from Hamburg, across the river from Bolonia, and only a stone's throw from Frankfurt. Geographically it has the basic shape of a question mark.

Hotdogastan is world-renowned for three major reasons:

First, the original Garden of Eden is located within its borders. "The Garden" is open Monday through Friday for locals and tourists. The inhabitants of Hotdogastan visit the Garden of Eden frequently for weddings, birthday parties, and local soccer tournaments. On Saturday it is open exclusively for animals, and on Sundays the Garden is reserved for the one and only Unicorn.

The second claim to fame for Hotdogastan is that it is the only country in the world where every citizen receives a copy of *A Teenager's Compass to Life* when they reach the age of 13. That copy becomes a lifetime treasure, and people from Hotdogastan cherish their personal copy until the end of their days.

The third noteworthy attribute of Hotdogastan is that once a year the nation hosts *"The Festival of Teens."* This is an annual three-day celebration, held in the Garden of Eden and presided over by Izzi Tooinsky, the king of the country. On the Saturday night of the festival, after the dancing and singing have subsided, all the teens make their way to the highest knoll in the Garden of Eden, where they sit with the king. While sipping frothy mugs of hot chocolate under a canopy of stars, the king and the teens discuss, argue, and ponder the proverbs, sayings, quotes and jokes written in this ancient manuscript which you now hold in your hands.

How to Use This Book

A Teenager's Compass to Life is a compilation of classic and modern quotes, jokes, sayings, and proverbs, which have been written or spoken by some of history's greatest poets, comedians, teachers, and fools.

It is highly recommended by the sages of Hotdogastan that you keep this book within easy reach, preferably next to your bed. They suggest you use it as a reference for when you're curious about a particular human experience, or whenever you're seeking a little personal clarity, or in those moments when you need some good old-fashioned common sense. That's the purpose of this book. It brings the wisdom of the age right to you, whoever and wherever you are.

As you read this book, you'll become more familiar with the quoted authors, and they'll begin to feel like wonderful old friends walking the path of life alongside you. The more you refer to this book, the more it will become like a personal compass that will help you navigate the peaks and valleys of life, guiding you to more happiness, more humor, more strength, and more wisdom.

The Ever-Changing Book

Each generation of teenagers in Hotdogastan, and beyond, has the joy and obligation to personally add NEW quotes, sayings, proverbs, and jokes to the book. This keeps the manuscript constantly alive and filled with vitality, century after century.

Here's how you can add to the book:

Located at the end of the text you will find 10 lined pages. When you hear someone say a particularly insightful statement, or when you read a quote that you want to savor, or when someone tells you a joke you don't want to forget, write it in the last 10 pages of your book. You can also send them to me at teencompass1@gmail.com. In both of those ways, you will become a coauthor in this unique, ancient manuscript.

Now... Welcome to: *A Teenager's Compass to Life.*

Pointing the Way

A

Accepting Others

When you love someone, you love the person as they are and not as you'd like them to be.

- Leo Tolstoy, Russian Author, 1828-1910

Accepting Mistakes

Even the greatest scribe makes a little smudge sometimes.

- Egyptian Proverb

Accepting and Letting Go

Not my circus, not my monkeys.

- Russian Proverb

Acceptance & Expectation

Serenity comes when you trade expectations for acceptance.

- Gautama Buddha, Founder of Buddhism, 563 - 480 BCE

Adventure &

Self Knowledge

It is only in adventure that some people succeed in knowing themselves.

- Andre Gide, French Author, 1889-1951

Accomplishing The Greatest

To be yourself in a world that is constantly trying to make you something else is the greatest accomplishment.

- Ralph Waldo Emerson, American Philosopher, 1803-1882

Adventure and Your Pocket

Nothing makes a man so adventurous as an empty pocket.

- Victor Hugo, French Author,1802-1885

Advice From Fools

Every fool wants to give advice.

- Italian Proverb

Advice to Myself

I give myself very good advice, but I very seldom follow it.

- Lewis Carroll, English Author, 1832-1898

Advising Others ?

I have found the best way to give advice to your children is to find out what they want and then advise them to do it.

- Harry S. Truman, 33rd President of the United States, 1884-1972

Alien Life

How many inhabitable planets are there? Astronomers estimate that there are approximately 50 billion planets in our Milky Way Galaxy alone. Of these planets, at least 500 million may be inhabitable.

- Carlos Roan, Brazilian Astronomer, 1940-1990

Alien Joke

Q. How did the space alien keep his pants up?

A. With an asteroid belt.

- Richie's Great Big Chicago Joke Book

Alone With Your Ideas

Be alone. That is the secret of invention; be alone, that is when ideas are born.

- Nikola Tesla, Austrian/American Inventor and Futurist, 1856-1943

American Cooperation

My fellow Americans, ask not what your country can do for you - ask what you can do for your country.

- John F Kennedy, 35th President of the United States, 1917-1963

American Dream

The American Dream, plain and simple, is that anyone in our country, willing to work hard enough, has the opportunity to become financially successful.

- Sally Hape, Social Studies Teacher, Lincoln Nebraska

America: United We Stand

America will never be destroyed from the outside. If we falter and lose our freedoms, it will be because we destroyed ourselves.

- Abraham Lincoln, 16th President of the United States, 1809-1865

Animals & Us

Until one has loved an animal, a part of one's soul remains unawakened.

- Anatole France, French journalist, novelist, and poet, 1844-1924

Animals First

Practice love on animals first; they react better and more sensitively.

- George Gurdjieff, Armenian/Greek Philosopher and Mystic, 1866-1949

Animal Lover

Whoever loves me, also loves my dog.

- Saint Bernard of Clairvaux, French Priest and Mystic, 1090-1153

Anger

People always say they are angry. The truth is, underneath that anger is almost always hurt feelings.

- Ellen Chroman, Master Gardener, 1955-2020

Anger and Enemies

He who overcomes his anger overcomes his greatest enemy.

- Publilius Syrus, Syrian Author and Philosopher, 85-43 BCE

Anger and Patience

Remember, if somebody makes you mad, tell the person you will come back after twenty-four hours to answer him.

- George Gurdjieff, Armenian/Greek Philosopher and Mystic, 1866-1949

Anger Boils

It's impossible to see your reflection in boiling water. Just like that, you can't see the truth when you are stuck in anger.

- Paulette Mahurin, My Cousin and well-known author of *The Seven Year Dress* and many other novels

Anger Made by Sadness

Anger is a sadness that had nowhere to go for a very long time.

- Ellen Chroman, Master Gardener, 1955-2020

Anne Frank Joke

Anne Frank would be so pissed if she knew everyone was reading her diary.

- Isadoor Bell, Dutch Comedian

Answering Your Call

Even if you feel you've missed your calling, it's never too late to pick up the phone.

- Sean Sanford, Author of Manbaby Requiem, 1982-

Argue at Your Level

Never wrestle with pigs. You both get dirty, and the pig likes it.

- George Bernard Shaw, Irish Playwright, 1856-1950

Arguing with the Ignorant

It is better to be silent than to argue with the ignorant.

- Pythagoras, Greek Philosopher, 570-490 BCE

Arrogance and Humility

Let the one among you who is without sin be the first to cast a stone.

- Jesus of Nazareth, Preacher and Religious Leader, 6 BCE - 33

Art

Art is either plagiarism or revolution.

- Paul Gauguin, French Painter, 1848-1903

Art & Love

The more I think it over, the more I feel that there is nothing more truly artistic than to love people.

- Vincent Van Gogh, Dutch Painter, 1853-1890

Art and Souls

You use a mirror to see your face; you use works of art to see your soul.

- George Bernard Shaw, Irish Playwright, 1856-1950

Art is Forever

I paint flowers so they will not die.

- Frida Kahlo, Mexican Painter, 1907-1954

Art of Living

The art of living requires a delicate balance between order and disorder, control and vulnerability.

- Rosalind Annenberg, Award Winning Addiction Educator, Los Angeles, CA

Artists Ask Questions

The role of the artist is to ask questions, not answer them.

- Anton Chekhov, Russian Author, 1860-1904

Art's Purpose

Art is not a mirror to hold up to reality. It's a hammer with which to shape it.

- Bertoit Brecht, German Playwright, 1898-1956

Asking for Help

The squeaky wheel gets the grease.

- English Proverb

Attention to Life

Wake up! Pay attention! That simple act will make you more alive, happier, and smarter.

- Henri-Louis Bergson, French Nobel Prize Winner for Literature, 1859-1941

Attitude of the Tough

When the going gets tough, the tough get going.

- American Saying

Atrocities & Absurdities

Those who can be made to believe in absurdities can be made to commit atrocities.

- Voltaire, French Author and Philosopher, 1694-1778

Authority

Either you think – or else others think for you and take your power from you.

- F. Scott Fitzgerald, American Author, 1896-1940

Award Joke

Q. Why did the scarecrow win an award?

A. Because he was outstanding in his field.

- Richie's Great Big Chicago Joke Book

B

Bad Company

If you lay down with dogs, you'll get up with fleas.

- English Proverb

Balancing Life

Life is a game of constantly holding on and constantly letting go.

- Rūmī, Persian Mystic and Poet, 1207-1273

Bald Joke

Q. What did the bald man say when he got a comb for this birthday?

A. Thanks, I'll never part with this.

- Richie's Great Big Chicago Joke Book

Bear Joke

Q. What do you call a bear with bad teeth?

A. A gummy bear

- Richie's Great Big Chicago Joke Book

Beard Joke

I didn't like my beard at first. Then it grew on me.

- Richie's Great Big Chicago Joke Book

Beauty Fades

Beauty is a short-lived tyranny.

- Socrates, Greek Philosopher, 469-399 BCE

Bee Joke

Q. Why do bees hum?

A. Because they forgot the words.

- Courtney and Marni Luxford, Authors of Bees, Birds, and Bison

Begin Well

Well begun is half done.

- Aristotle, Greek Philosopher, 384-322 BCE

Beginning the Journey

A journey of a thousand miles must begin with a single step.

- Lao Tzu, Legendary Chinese Philosopher, 604-531 BCE

Beginning to Try

Every giant oak tree started as a tiny nut that just kept on trying.

- English Parable

Be Yourself

Be yourself. Everyone else is taken.

- Oscar Wilde, Irish Playwright and Poet, 1854-1900

Bible Talk

The devil can cite scripture for his own purpose.

- William Shakespeare, English Playwright 1564-1616

Birth and Tears

When we are born, we cry because we have come to this great stage of fools.

- William Shakespeare, English Playwright, 1564-1616

Blabbermouth

You speak an infinite deal of nothing.

- William Shakespeare, English Playwright, 1564-1616

Blabbermouth All the Time

A dog that barks all the time gets little attention.

- Argentinian Proverb

Blabbermouth and a Drum

An empty drum gives the loudest sound.

- Indonesian Proverb

Blame is Easy

To blame is easy, to do it better is difficult.

- German Proverb

Blessed by Friendship

May you always be blessed with the gift of true friendship.

- Steve Clements, My Old Buddy from Hotdogastan

Blockheads Compared

A learned blockhead is a greater blockhead than an ignorant one.

- Ben Franklin, Inventor, Printer, and Political Philosopher, 1706-1790

Boldness

Fortune favors the bold.

- Virgil, Roman Poet, 71-20 BCE

Boldness & Calamity

Yield not to calamity but face her boldly.

- Virgil, Roman Poet, 71-20 BCE

Boldness Joke

Q. *What did the shy pebble say?*

A. *I wish I was a little bolder.*

- Richie's Great Big Chicago Joke Book

Book Joke

I'm reading a book about anti-gravity. It's impossible to put down!

- Richie's Great Big Chicago Joke Book

Broken People

It is easier to build strong children than to repair broken men.

- Frederick Douglass, African American Social Reformer, Statesman, 1818-1895

Busy Life

Beware the barrenness of a busy life.

- Socrates, Greek Philosopher, 469-399 BCE

C

Car Joke

Last night I had a dream that I was a muffler. I woke up exhausted.

- Richie's Great Big Chicago Joke Book

Care is Felt

People don't care how much you know until they know how much you care.

- Theodore Roosevelt, 26th President, 1858-1919

Careful with Insults

Never insult an alligator until you have successfully crossed the river.

- Jamaican Parable

Cash Joke

Knock knock. Who's there?

Cash. Cash who?

No thanks, but how about some walnuts.

- Richie's Great Big Chicago Joke Book

Cats Can Improve People

Of all God's creatures, there is only one that cannot be beaten into submission. That one is the cat. If man could be crossed with the cat it would improve the man, but it would deteriorate the cat.

- Mark Twain, American Author, 1835-1910

Cat Proverbs

I gave an order to a cat, and the cat gave it to its tail. – China

The man who loves cats will love his wife. – Russia

A house without a dog or cat is the house of a scoundrel. - Portugal

Caution with Genies

Once you've let the genie out, it's hard to get it back in the bottle.

- Dutch Proverb

Celebrities & Loneliness

It is strange to be known so universally and yet to be so lonely.

- Albert Einstein, German-born Theoretical Physicist, 1879-1955

Cell Phone Prophecy in 1926

Within a few years a simple and inexpensive device, readily carried about, will enable one to receive on land or sea the ... news, to hear a speech, a lecture, a song or play of a musical instrument, conveyed from any other region of the globe.

- Nikola Tesla, Austrian/American Inventor and Futurist, 1856-1943

Certainty: There's Only One

There is only one certainty in life, and that is that nothing is certain.

- G.K. Chesterton, English Philosopher, 1874-1936

Challenge of Rising

Our greatest glory is not in never failing but in rising up every time we fail.

- Confucius, Chinese Philosopher, 551 - 479 BCE

Challenges and Calmness

A ship doesn't travel far in a calm sea.

- Moroccan Proverb

Challenges Make Us Skillful

Smooth seas do not make skillful sailors.

- Kenyan Proverb

Challenges & Opposition

Great spirits have often encountered violent opposition from weak minds.

- Albert Einstein, German-born Theoretical Physicist, 1879-1955

Challenging Opportunity

In the middle of difficulty lies opportunity.

- Albert Einstein, German-born Theoretical Physicist, 1879-1955

Change

Just as a snake sheds its skin, we must shed our past over and over again.

- Gautama Buddha, Founder of Buddhism, 563 - 480 BCE

Changes

Be the change that you wish to see in the world.

- Mahatma Gandhi, Nonviolent Anti Colonialist, Politician, 1869-1948

Change Your Mind

A wise person changes their mind. A fool never will.

- Spanish Proverb

Change Yourself

Everyone thinks of changing the world, but no one thinks of changing himself.

- Leo Tolstoy, Russian Author, 1828-1910

Changing Can Hurt

Change is like a new pair of shoes. Sometimes they hurt at first, but eventually, they become your favorite.

- Penny el-Akkad, Shoe Saleswoman in Auburn California

Character is What is Left

Character is what is left after everything you can buy, borrow, acquire or fake is taken away.

- Booker T. Washington, Civil Rights Activist and Educator, 1856-1915

Character's True Test

The true measure of a person's character is how they treat those who can do nothing for them.

- Baal Shem Tov, Jewish Mystic and Healer, 1668-1760

Cheap & Expensive

The cheapest is always the most expensive.

- German Proverb

Chicken Joke

Q. What compliment did the handsome rooster give the lovely chicken?

A. You are impeccable.

- Richie's Great Big Chicago Joke Book

Child Rearing

Child rearing is a delicate balance between tolerance and setting boundaries.

- Rosalind Annenberg, Award-Winning Addiction Educator, Los Angeles, CA

Children in the Center

Let us all resolve to put children at the center of all we do. They must be the motivation for every decision we make.

- *Nelson Mandela, President of South Africa and Freedom Fighter, 1918-2013*

Children and History

History will judge us by the difference we make in the everyday lives of children.

- Nelson Mandela, President of South Africa and Freedom Fighter, 1918- 2013

Children are Fast

The fastest land animal on the planet is a toddler with a spoon in his mouth.

- Thea Chroman, Working Mom, Eldest of my 12 daughters.

Children are Jewels

The most precious jewels you'll ever have around your neck are the arms of children.

- Janice Powers, Gardening Aficionado, 1957-

Children Heal

The soul is healed by being with children.

- Janice Powers, Gardening Aficionado, 1957-

Children Laugh More

The average kid laughs 400 times a day. The average adult, 11.

- *Laurel Canyon, School Therapist, Santa Monica, CA*

Children: Love and Freedom

Receive the children in reverence, educate them in love, and send them forth in freedom.

- Rudolf Steiner, Austrian Social Reformer and Architect, 1861-1925

Children's Message

Every child comes with the message that God is not yet discouraged by man.

- Rabindranath Tagore, Indian Playwright and Poet, 1861-1941

Children's Naughtiness

It's not attention that the child is seeking, but love.

- Sigmund Freud, Austrian Founder of Psychoanalysis, 1856-1939

Citizen of the World

I am not an Athenian or a Greek. I am a citizen of the world.

- Socrates, Greek Philosopher, 469-399 BCE

Civilization, Rocks, and Words

Civilization began the first time an angry person cast a word instead of a rock.

- Sigmund Freud, Austrian Founder of Psychoanalysis, 1856-1939

Clothes & Nakedness

Clothes make the man. Naked people have little or no influence on society.

- *Mark Twain, American Author, 1835-1910*

Clown Joke

Yesterday, a clown held the door open for me. It was such a nice jester!

- Richie's Great Big Chicago Joke Book

Colorful Joke

I just found out I'm colorblind. The diagnosis came completely out of the purple.

- Richie's Great Big Chicago Joke Book

Comedy & Paradise

The person who makes his companions laugh deserves paradise.

- Mohammad, Founder of Islam, 570-632

Comedy Teaches

The duty of comedy is to inform people by amusing them.

- Moliere, French playwright, 1622-1673

Common Sense & Genius

Common sense is genius dressed up in its working clothes.

- Ralph Waldo Emerson, American Philosopher, 1803-1882

Common Sense

God is good, but don't dance in a small boat.

- Nigerian Proverb

Communication, Listen More

We have two ears and one mouth. That's so that we can listen twice as much as we speak.

- Epictetus, Greek Philosopher, 50-138

Community Effort

If each person sweeps before his own door, the whole street is clean.

- Irish Proverb

Companions and You

A person is known by the company he keeps.

- Greek Saying

Compassion is the Answer

If we truly knew what was in each person's history, compassion would be the answer to every issue.

- Rosalind Annenberg, Award Winning Addiction Educator, Los Angeles, CA

Complaining About the Band

The girl who can't dance says the band can't play.

- Yiddish Proverb

Complaining Fool

Any fool can criticize, condemn, and complain—and most fools do.

- Dale Carnegie, American Author and Lecturer, 1888-1955

Complaining or Working

An inch of progress is worth more than a yard of complaint.

- Booker T. Washington, Civil Rights Activist and Educator, 1856-1915

Compliment

Is there an airport nearby, or is that just my heart taking off?

- Cliff Notez, Salsa Dancing Instructor, Phoenix Arizona

Compliment: 1 to 10

On a scale from one to ten, you're an eleven.

- Cliff Notez, Salsa Dancing Instructor, Phoenix Arizona

Compliment about Sparkling

Excuse me, but do you have something in your eye?

Oh, now I see. It's just a permanent sparkle.

- Candice Sanford Nobles, C.E.O. of Efin Relax

Complimentary Thief

You're a great thief. You stole my heart in a second.

- Cliff Notez, Salsa Dancing Instructor, Phoenix Arizona

Computer Cat Joke

Q. Why do cats like to stay near the computers?

A. So they can keep an eye on the mouse.

- Richie's Great Big Chicago Joke Book

Conceit

The smaller the mind, the greater the conceit.

- Aesop, Greek Slave and Storyteller, 620-556 BCE

Confidence

You haven't seen anything yet!

- Miguel de Cervantes, Spanish Author, 1547-161

Conscience Without Fear

The safest course is to do nothing against your own conscience. With this secret, we can enjoy life and have no fear of death.

- Voltaire, French Author and Philosopher, 1694-1778

Conquer Yourself

It is better to conquer yourself than to win a thousand battles. If you do that, the victory is yours. It cannot be taken from you.

- Gautama Buddha, Founder of Buddhism, 563 - 480 BCE

Contentment is Rich

He who is content is rich.

- Lao Tzu, Legendary Chinese Philosopher, 604-531 BCE

Contentment With What You Have?

If a person is not content with what they have, they will not be content with what they would like to have.

- Socrates, Greek Philosopher, 469-399 BCE

Contribute or Die

When you cease to make a contribution, you begin to die.

- Eleanor Roosevelt, First Lady of the U.S. between 1944 and 1945, 1884-1962

Convictions Can Seem Absurd

Listen to your convictions, even if they seem absurd to your reason.

- Found in the Egyptian Temple of Luxor

Cooking Joke

If God wanted me to cook, why did he invent restaurants?

- Richie's Great Big Chicago Joke Book

Country and Religion

My country is the world, and my religion is to do good.

- Thomas Paine, English-born American Political Activist and Philosopher, 1737-1809

Courage

Take courage, my heart: you have been through worse than this.

- Homer, Greek Poet, 8th Century BCE

Courage and Caring

From caring comes courage.

- Lao Tzu, Legendary Chinese Philosopher, 604-531 BCE

Courage & Strength

Courage isn't having the strength to go on- it's going on when you don't have the strength.

- Napoleon Bonaparte, French Emperor and Military Commander, 1769-1821

Courage Comes From Loving

Being deeply loved by someone gives you strength, while loving someone deeply gives you courage.

- Lao Tzu, Legendary Chinese Philosopher, 604-531 B

Courage, Especially When You are Scared

Courage means being scared to death, but doing what you need to anyway.

- Ellen Chroman, Master Gardener, 1955-2020

Courage First

Courage is the first of human qualities because it is the quality that guarantees others.

- Aristotle, Greek Philosopher, 384-322 BCE

Courageous Creativity

Creativity takes courage.

- Henri Matisse, French Artist, 1869-1954

Courage to Love

It takes a great deal of courage to see the world in all its tainted glory, and still to love it.

- Oscar Wilde, Irish Playwright and Poet, 1854-1900

Courage to Show

It takes a lot of courage to show your dreams to someone else.

- Ellen Chroman, Master Gardener, 1955-2020

Courage to Stand Alone

It's easy to stand with a crowd. It takes courage to stand alone.

- Mahatma Gandhi, Nonviolent Anti Colonialist, Politician, 1869-1948

Courage and Critics

Whatever you do, you need courage. Whatever course you decide upon, there is always someone to tell you that you are wrong. There are always difficulties arising that tempt you to believe your critics are right.

- Ralph Waldo Emerson, American Philosopher, 1803-1882

Cowardly Choices

To see the right way and not to do it is cowardice.

- Confucius, Chinese Philosopher, 551-479 BCE

Cowardly Man

A guy who encourages the love of a woman just to get her to open up to him sexually is the worst kind of coward.

- Leroy Johnson, Owned a fruit truck in Inglewood CA in the 1970's

Crazy Act

When all else fails

pretend you're crazy.

- Tunisian Proverb

Crazy Cheese

His cheese has slipped off his crackers.

- American Proverb

Craziness Everywhere

You're entirely bonkers. But I'll tell you a secret... All the best people are!

- Lewis Carroll, English Author, 1832-1898

Creative Bumbling

That's the way it is with fools. You can bumble your way to wonder.

- Marty Graw, Comedia Del Arte Performer, Oakland California

Climate Crisis

Our house is on fire. I'm here to say that our house is on fire.

- Greta Thunberg Swedish, Political Activist, 2003-

Crime and Punishment

One of the tests of the civilization of people is the treatment of its criminals.

- Rutherford B. Hayes, 19th President of America, 1822-1893

Criticism

Criticism is something we can avoid easily by saying nothing, doing nothing, and being nothing.

- Aristotle, Greek Philosopher, 384-322 BCE

Critics and Genius

The dread of criticism is the death of genius.

- William Gilmore Simms, Novelist and Historian, 1800-1879

Critics Beware

People who live in glass houses shouldn't throw stones.

- English Proverb

Criticism Happens

Do what you feel in your heart to be right, for you'll be criticized anyway.

- Eleanor Roosevelt, First Lady of the U.S. between 1944 and 1945, 1884-1962

Criticizing - Self Boasting

Criticism is an indirect form of self-boasting.

- Emmit Fox, Irish Religious Leader, 1886-1951

Critical of your neighbor?

Do not judge your neighbor until you walk two moons in his moccasins.

- Cheyenne Teaching

Critical Source

When you are being criticized, consider the source.

- Rosalind Annenberg, *Award-Winning* Addiction Educator, Los Angeles, CA

Criticism Joke

Before you criticize a man, walk a mile in his shoes, that way, when you are done criticizing him, you'll be a mile away and you'll have his shoes.

- Michael Barns Alaskan Radio Personality, 1925-1969

Crying and the Soul

What soap is for the body, tears are for the soul.

- Jewish Proverb

Crying Can Help

Don't be afraid to cry. It will free your mind of sorrowful thoughts.

- Hopi Teaching

Curse of Beauty

May your daughter's beauty be admired by everyone in the circus.

- Yiddish Proverb

Curse of Dancers

May your enemies get cramps in their legs while they are dancing on your grave.

- Yiddish Proverb

Curse That Stinks

I hope you swallow boiled farts.

- William Shakespeare, English Playwright, 1564-1616

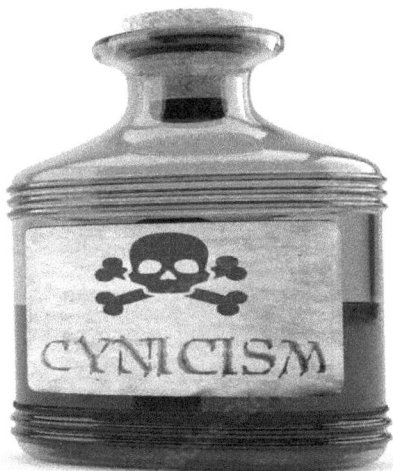

Cynics, Prices, and Value

A cynic is a man who knows the price of everything and the value of nothing.

- Oscar Wilde, Irish Playwright and Poet, 1854-1900

D

Dancing Joke

I was addicted to the hokey pokey... but thankfully, I turned myself around.

- Richie's Great Big Chicago Joke Book

Danger of Doing Nothing

The world is a dangerous place to live, not because of the people who are evil, but because of the people who don't do anything about it.

- Albert Einstein, German-born Theoretical Physicist, 1879-1955

Danger Avoided

Avoiding danger is no safer in the long run than outright exposure. Life is either a daring adventure or nothing.

- Helen Keller, Author, Disability Rights Advocate, 1880-1968

Darkest Times

It is during our darkest moments that we must focus to see the light.

- Aristotle, Greek Philosopher, 384-322 BCE

Dark Side of Your Moon

Everyone is a moon and has a dark side he never shows to anybody.

- *Mark Twain, American Author, 1835-1910*

Dating Recommendation

What to look for when you are dating someone.

You want to feel free, strong, and safe when you are with them. If that's not happening, let it go.

- Rosey Fernandes, After School Programs for Teenagers, Sacramento CA.

Death

Death may be the greatest of all human blessings.

Socrates, Greek Philosopher

469-399 BC E

Death and Taxes

In this world, nothing can be certain except for death and taxes.

- Ben Franklin, Inventor, Printer, and Political Philosopher, 1706-1790

Death and Status

In the end, the king and the pawn get put in the same box.

- Italian Proverb

Death Comes

Every person knows that they must die, but they just don't believe it.

- German Saying

Death of Socrates

The hour of departure has arrived, and we go our separate ways, I to die, and you to live. Which of these two is better, only God knows.

- Socrates, Greek Philosopher, 469-399 BCE

Death Probability

I would have to say the probability of us dying seems extremely high.

- Pythagoras, Greek Philosopher, 570-490 BCE

Death Reports

The reports of my death have been greatly exaggerated.

Mark Twain, American Author, 1835-1910

Death Joke

I want to die peacefully in my sleep, like my grandfather. Not screaming and yelling like the other passengers in his car.

- Will Rogers, American Humorist, 1879-1935

Death Joke 2

R.I.P boiled water. You will be mist.

- Richie's Great Big Chicago Joke Book

Defend It or Lose It

Life isn't worth living unless you are forced to defend it every once and a while.

- Lakota Saying

Degrading Others

Whoever degrades another degrades me.

- Walt Whitman, American Poet, 1819-1892

Destiny

Watch your thoughts, they become your words.

Watch your words, they become your actions.

Watch your actions, they become your habits.

Watch your habits, they become your character.

Watch your character, it becomes your destiny.

- Lao Tzu, Legendary Chinese Philosopher, 604-531 BCE

Depression

I'm currently in the middle of a depression. I couldn't really tell you what set it off, but I think it stems from my cowardice, which confronts me at every turn.

- Anne Frank, German-born, Jewish Holocaust Victim, 1929-1945

Depression Therapy

One of the best therapies I have found for the problem of depression is to let a puppy lick your face. Do this daily for one week. I've seen it work miracles.

- Charleen Lambond, Cuddle with Love, Animal Thrift Store, Volunteer, Nickelsville Maine

Desire

There are two tragedies in life. One is to lose your heart's desire. The other is to gain it.

- George Bernard Shaw, Irish Playwright, 1856-1950

Desire

Be suspicious of what you think you want.

- Rumi, Islamic Poet and Mystic, 1207-1273

Determined to Succeed

Don't worry. It's often the last key in the bunch that opens the door.

- Morrie Chroman, L and M Plumbing, Los Angeles CA., 1926-2007

Devils are Here!

Hell is empty, and all the devils are here.

- William Shakespeare, English Playwright 1564-1616

Devil's Lips

Satan's successes are the greatest when he appears with the name of God on his lips.

- Mahatma Gandhi, Nonviolent Anti Colonialist, Politician, 1869-1948

Devil and Eden

We are our own devils; we drive ourselves out of our Edens.

- Johann Wolfgang von Goethe, German Author, 1749-1832

Dignity of Begging

There is something to be said for anyone who sits alone with dignity and silently begs for God.

- Rumi, Islamic Poet and Mystic, 1207-1273

Dignity Undeserved

Let none presume to wear an undeserved dignity.

- William Shakespeare, English Playwright 1564-1616

Diligently Walking

The path is made by walking.

- African Proverb

Diligence: Drop by Drop

Drop by drop, you break the rock.

- Māori Proverb

Discover Yourself

The best way to find yourself is to lose yourself in the service of others.

- Mahatma Gandhi, Nonviolent Anti Colonialist, Politician, 1869-1948

Discoveries Take Courage

Man cannot discover new oceans unless he has the courage to lose sight of the shore.

- Andre Gide, French Author, 1889-1951

Disease and Food

Treat all diseases through food and diet. If that doesn't work, try other means.

- Maimonides, Spanish/Egyptian Talmudist, Physician, and Philosopher, 1138-1204

Disease

It is far more important to know what person the disease has, than what disease the person has.

- Hippocrates, Greek Physician, 460-370 BCE

Diversity is Wonderful

It takes many kinds of flowers to make a full and vibrant bouquet.

- Arabic Proverb

DNA Joke

Q. What did one DNA molecule say to the other DNA molecule?

A. Do these genes make me look fat?

- Richie's Great Big Chicago Joke Book

Doctor Yourself

If you are not your own doctor, you are a fool.

- Hippocrates, Greek Physician, 460-370 BCE

Dogs

Outside of a dog, a book is a man's best friend. Inside of a dog, it's too dark to read.

- Groucho Marx, American Comedian, 1890-1977

Dogs and People

The more I learn about people, the more I like my dog.

- Mark Twain, American Author, 1835-1910

Dogs Do or Don't Like You?

If a dog will not come to you after having looked you in the face, you should go home and examine your conscience.

- Woodrow Wilson, 28th President of the United States, 1856-1924

Dog Joke

Q. What type of a dog did the chemist have?

A. A lab!

- Richie's Great Big Chicago Joke Book

Dog Joke 2

Q. What did the dog say after he ate sandpaper?

A. Ruff

- Lady Powers, *The Canine Comedian, Penn Valley CA.*

Dog Joke 3

My wife asked me if I had seen the dog bowl,
and I answered, "I didn't know that it could."

- Richie's Great Big Chicago Joke Book

Do It Yourself

The trouble with life is, that you're halfway through life before you realize that it's a Do-It-Yourself thing.

- *Jack Cheese, Gardener and Handy Man, Fairbanks Alaska*

Doubt and Wisdom

Doubt is the beginning of wisdom.

- Rene Descartes, French Philosopher and Scientist, 1596-1650

Dreaming is Good

If you have built castles in the air, your work need not be lost; that is where they should be. Now put the foundations under them.

- Henry David Thoreau, American Philosopher, 1817-1862

Dreams Come True

Dreams can come true, but there is a secret. They're realized through the magic of persistence, determination, commitment, passion, practice, focus and hard work. They happen a step at a time, manifested over years, not weeks.

- Elbert Hubbard, American Author and Philosopher, 1856-1915

Dream Joke

Keep the dream alive — hit your snooze button.

- Kari Oki, Jokester at the Oregon Country Fair, 1982

Drinking and Swimming

I tried to drown my sorrows, but the bastards learned to swim.

- Frida Kahlo, Mexican Painter, 1907-1954

Dying Scares Me

It is not death; it is dying that scares me.

- Michel de Montaigne, French Philosopher, 1513-159

E

Earth Provides

The Earth provides enough to satisfy every person's needs, but not enough for every person's greed.

- Mahatma Gandhi, Nonviolent Anti Colonialist, Politician, 1869-1948

Educated Person

It is the mark of an educated mind to be able to entertain a thought without accepting it.

- Aristotle, Greek Philosopher, 384-322 BCE

Education and Schooling

I never let my schooling get in the way of my education.

- Mark Twain, American Author, 1835-1910

Education of the Youth

All who have meditated on the art of governing people have been convinced that the fate of empires depends on the education of its youth.

- Aristotle, Greek Philosopher, 384-322 BCE

Education: Mind and Heart

Educating the mind without educating the heart is no education at all.

- Aristotle, Greek Philosopher, 384-322 BCE

Education; Be Involved

Tell me, and I forget. Teach me, and I remember.

Involve me, and I learn.

- Ben Franklin, Inventor, Printer, and Political Philosopher, 1706-1790

Education or Not

You can lead a horse to water, but you can't make it drink.

- American Proverb

Effort and Honey

No bees, no honey. No work, no money.

- Jamaican Proverb

Electrical Joke

Most people are shocked when they find out how bad I am as an electrician.

- Richie's Great Big Chicago Joke Book

Emotional Slavery

Any person capable of angering you becomes your master.

- Epictetus, Greek Philosopher, 50-138

Emotions Show on the Face

For news of the heart, ask the face.

- West African Proverb

Emotion and Sorrow

Every man has his secret sorrows which the world knows not, and often we call that man cold, when really, he is only sad.

- Henry Wadsworth Longfellow, American Poet, 1807-1882

End of Days Joke

In the end of days, the lion and the calf shall lie down together… but the calf won't get much sleep.

- Woody Allen, American Film maker, Author, Comedian 1935-

Enemies Become Friends

The best way to destroy an enemy is to make him a friend.

- Abraham Lincoln, 16th President of the United States, 1809-1865

Enemies and your Faults

Love your Enemies, for they tell you your faults.

- Ben Franklin, Inventor, Printer, and Political Philosopher, 1706-1790

Enemies with Wisdom

A wise enemy is better than a foolish friend.

- Afghan Saying

Energy of a Raisin

The energy in a raisin could light up all of New York City if it moved at the speed of light.

- Albert Einstein, German-born Theoretical Physicist, 1879-1955

Errors Lead to Discoveries

In man's errors are his portals of discovery.

- James Joyce, Irish Author, 1882-1941

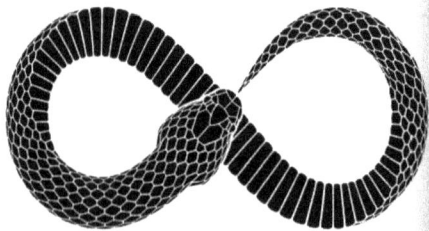

Eternity

How long is eternity?

A white eagle drags a piece of green silk over a craggy mountain once every 1000 years. The amount of time it takes to wear the mountain flat... is an eternity.

- Noah Zark, Storyteller at the Renaissance Faire, Agoura CA. 1973

Evil & Good

If good men do nothing, evil will prevail.

- Edmund Burke, Irish/English Philosopher and Statesman, 1729-1797

Exercise Joke

I just burned 2,000 calories. That's the last time I leave brownies in the oven while I nap.

- Richie's Great Big Chicago Joke Book

Expectations

A great man is hard on himself.

A weak man is hard on others.

- Confucius, Chinese Philosopher, 551 - 479 BCE

Expectations & Heartache

Expectation is the root of all heartache.

- William Shakespeare, English Playwright 1564-1616

Experience/Mistakes

Experience is merely the name men give to their mistakes.

- Oscar Wilde, Irish Playwright and Poet, 1854-1900

Excuses or Changes

Make excuses or make changes. The choice is yours.

- Ann Knotter, British Author, 1945-1999

Excusing Yourself and Others?

I attribute my success to this,

I never gave or took any excuse.

- Florence Nightingale, Mother of Modern Nursing, 1820-1910

Explore, Dream, Discover

Twenty years from now, you will be more disappointed by the things that you didn't do than by the ones you did do. So, throw off the bowlines. Sail away from the safe harbor. Catch the trade winds in your sails. Explore. Dream. Discover.

- Mark Twain, American Author, 1835-1910

Exploring the Limbs

Why not go out on a limb? Isn't that where the fruit is?

- Mark Twain, American Author, 1835-1910

F

Failure and Success

I have not failed. I've just found 10,000 ways that won't work.

- Thomas A. Edison, American Inventor, 1847-1931

Falling in Love

Falling in love and having a relationship are two different things.

- Janice Powers, Gardening Aficionado, 1957-

Fame and Peace

Fame and peace can never be best friends.

- Michel de Montaigne, French Philosopher, 1513-1592

Fame & Stupidity

With fame, I become more and more stupid, which of course, is a very common phenomenon.

- Albert Einstein, German-born Theoretical Physicist, 1879-1955

Fame Exposes

The higher a monkey climbs, the easier it is to see its behind.

- Costa Rican Proverb

Families: Sweet and Nutty

Families are like fudge, mostly sweet with a few nuts.

- American Saying

Family Love

The best action you can take to make the world a better place, is to go home and love your family.

- Amos Bronson Alcott, American Teacher and Philosopher, 1799-1888

Family Skeleton

If you cannot get rid of the family skeleton, you might as well make it dance.

- George Bernard Shaw, Irish Playwright, 1856-1950

Family Possibilities

Where love reigns, the impossible may be attained.

- Indian Proverb

Family Tree

The apple doesn't fall far from the tree.

- *English Proverb*

Famous Last Words

I have offended God and mankind because my work did not reach the quality it should have.

- Leonardo Da Vinci, Italian Artist,

  1451-1519

Famous Last Words

A dying man can do nothing easily.

- Ben Franklin, Inventor, Printer, and Political Philosopher, 1706-1790

Famous Last Words

I am content.

- John Quincy Adams, 6th President of U.S.A, 1767-1848

Famous Last Words

Pardon me, Sir, I did not do it on purpose.

(She stepped on the executioner's toes.}

- Marie Antoinette, Queen of France, 1755-1793

Famous Last Words

My wallpaper and I are fighting a duel to the death. One or the other of us has got to go.

- Oscar Wilde, Irish Playwright and Poet, 1854-1900

Famous Last   Words

I hope the exit is joyful and I hope never to return.

- Frida Kahlo, Mexican Painter, 1907-1954

Famous Last Words

I'll be fine.

- Heath Ledger, Australian Actor, 1979-2008

Famous Last Words

It is tasteless to prolong life artificially. I have done my share; it is time to go. I will do it elegantly.

- Albert Einstein, German-born Theoretical Physicist, 1879-1955

Famous Last Words

On his deathbed, Henry David Thoreau was asked if he had made his peace with God. He answered, "I didn't know that we had quarreled."

- Noah Zark, Storyteller at the Renaissance Faire, Agoura CA. 1973

Famous Last Words

Work hard to gain your own salvation.

- Gautama Buddha, Founder of Buddhism, 563 - 480 BCE

Famous Last Words

It is very beautiful over there.

- Thomas A. Edison, American Inventor, 1847-1931

Famous Last Words

If this is dying, it's not that big of a deal.

- Greg Lesson's Grandfather

Fanatics Can't Change

A fanatic is one who can't change his mind and won't change the subject.

- Winston Churchill, English Author and Politician, 1847-1965

Farming for Washington

I would rather be on my farm than be emperor of the world.

- George Washington, 1ˢᵗ President of the United States, 1732-1799

Fasting

What the eyes are for the outer world, fasts are for the inner.

- Mahatma Gandhi, Nonviolent Anti Colonialist, Politician, 1869-1948

Fasting as Medicine

The best of all medicines is rest and fasting.

- Ben Franklin, Inventor, Printer, and Political Philosopher, 1706-1790

Fasting is Easy

When the stomach is full, it's easy to speak of fasting.

- St Jerome, Christian Saint, Died 420

Father Joke

Today my son asked me, 'Can I have a bookmark'? I couldn't believe it. He's 12 years old and still doesn't know my name!

- Richie's Great Big Chicago Joke Book

Father Joke

Q. What did the buffalo say to his son when he dropped him off at school?

A. Bi-son.

- Richie's Great Big Chicago Joke Book

Father's Example

Every father needs to remember the fact that one day his sons will follow his example, not his advice.

- Jeremy Bentham, English Philosopher, 1748-1832

Father's Example 2

What the goat does, the kid follows.

Jamaican Proverb

Fathers Growing Old

To a father growing old, nothing is dearer than a daughter.

- Euripides, Greek Playwright, 485-403 BCE

Father's Protection

I cannot think of any need in childhood as strong as the need for a father's protection.

- Sigmund Freud, Austrian Founder of Psychoanalysis, 1856-1939

Faultless Friends

If you are looking for a friend who is faultless, you will be friendless.

- Rumi, Islamic Poet and Mystic, 1207-1273

Fear

The only thing we have to fear is fear itself.

- Franklin D. Roosevelt, 32nd President of the United States, 1882-1945

Fear and Passion

I am not afraid. I was born to do this.

- Joan of Arc, Defender of France, 1412-1431

Fear is Contagious

There is no passion more contagious than fear.

- Michel de Montaigne, French Philosopher, 1513-1592

Fear Practice

Do one thing each day that scares you.

- Eleanor Roosevelt, First Lady of the U.S. between 1933 and 1945, 1884-1962

Feeling Broken

It's pretty obvious and to their credit, that broken crayons still color.

- Leroy Johnson, Owned a fruit truck in Inglewood CA in the 1970's

Feelings and the Senses

The most beautiful things in the world cannot be seen or touched; they are felt with the heart.

- Antoine De Saint-Exupery, French Author and Aviation Pioneer, 1900-1944

Female Protection

The best protection any woman can have...is courage.

- Elizabeth Cady Stanton, Women's Rights Advocate, 1815-1902

Female Slavery

The prolonged slavery of women is the darkest page in human history.

- Elizabeth Cady Stanton, Women's Rights Advocate, 1815-1902

Fight

It's not the size of the dog in the fight. It's the size of the fight in the dog.

- Mark Twain, American Author, 1835-1910

Fighting for Life

Life is a hard battle. If we laugh and sing a little as we fight the good fight of freedom, it makes it all go easier. I will not allow my life's light to be determined by the darkness around me.

- Sojourner Truth, American Abolitionist, Died 1883

Finding Fault

If you limit your actions in life to things that nobody can possibly find fault with, you will not do much!

- Lewis Carroll, English Author, 1832-1898

Finding or Creating

Life isn't about finding yourself. Life is about creating yourself.

- George Bernard Shaw, Irish Playwright, 1856-1950

First Impressions

You never get a second chance to make a first impression.

- Will Rogers, American Humorist, 1879-1935

Flaws of Friends

Write in the sand the flaws of your friend.

- Pythagoras Greek Philosopher, 570-490 BCE

Focus or Lose It

The hunter in pursuit of an elephant does not stop to throw rocks at birds.

- Ugandan Proverb

Food and Death

We dig our graves with our forks.

- Italian Proverb

Food and Love

When love sets the table, the food tastes better.

- French Proverb

Food is Medicine

Our food should be our medicine and our medicine should be our food.

- Hippocrates, Greek Physician, 460-370 BCE

Food Joke

A guy walks into a restaurant. The hostess asks, "Do you have reservations?" The guy looks around and says "Sure, but I'll try your food anyway."

- Richie's Great Big Chicago Joke Book

Foolish

Stay hungry. Stay foolish.

- Steve Jobs, Co-Founded Apple Inc., 1955-2011

Fool is Wise?

A fool thinks himself to be wise, but a wise man knows himself to be a fool.

- William Shakespeare, English Playwright, 1564-1616

Fool Once a Month at Least

The cleverest of all, in my opinion, is the man who calls himself a fool at least once a month.

- Fyodor Dostoevsky, Russian Novelist, 1821-1881

Fool: Silent or Loud

Better to remain silent and be thought of as a fool than to speak out loud and remove all doubt.

- Abraham Lincoln, 16th President of the United States, 1809-1865

Fools and Evidence

No amount of evidence will ever persuade an idiot.

- Mark Twain, American Author, 1835-1910

Fools and Prophets

A whole fool is half a prophet.

- Jewish Proverb

Fools Everywhere

Foolery, sir, walks around the world like the sun. It shines everywhere.

- William Shakespeare, English Playwright 1564-1616

Fool's Mirror

Anyone who doesn't wish to see a fool should smash his mirror.

- Irish Proverb

Fool's Mission

Nothing is more dangerous than an idiot on a mission.

- Yiddish Proverb

Forgiveness is for the Strong

The weak can never forgive. Forgiveness is the attribute of the strong.

- Mahatma Gandhi, Nonviolent Anti Colonialist and Politician, 1869-1948

Forgive and Annoy

Always forgive your enemies; nothing annoys them so much.

- Oscar Wilde, Irish Playwright and Poet, 1854-1900

Freedom

No one is free who has not obtained the empire of himself.

- Pythagoras, Greek Philosopher, 570-490 BCE

Free Stuff

Free cheese can be found only in a mousetrap.

- Swiss Proverb

Free Will?

He who believes in freedom of the will has never loved and never hated.

- Marie Von Ebner-Eschenback, Austrian writer, 1830-1916

Friends & Ships

There are many types of ships. There are wooden ships and metal ships. But the best and most important types of ships are friendships.

- Irish Saying

Friendship's Gifts

Nothing opens the heart like a true friend, to whom you may impart griefs, joys, fears, hopes…and whatever lies upon the heart.

- Francis Bacon, English Philosopher and Statesman, 1561-1626

Friends Like You

Tell me who your friends are, so I can tell you who you are.

- Bulgarian Saying

Friends & Enemies

I don't like that man. I must get to know him better.

- Abraham Lincoln, 16th President of the United States, 1809-1865

Friendship Treasure

Whoever finds a faithful friend, finds a treasure.

- Jewish Saying

Frightful Ignorance

There is nothing more frightful than ignorance in action.

- Johann Wolfgang von Goethe, German Author, 1749-1832

Funniest People

The funniest people are the saddest ones.

- Confucius, Chinese Philosopher, 551 - 479 BCE

Futile Actions

You can't polish a turd.

- English Proverb

Future and the Present

The future depends on what we do in the present.

- Mahatma Gandhi, Nonviolent Anti Colonialist, Politician, 1869-1948

Future Folks

The strangest and sweetest songs yet remain to be sung.

- Walt Whitman, American Poet, 1819-1892

Future is Created Now!

The best way to predict the future is to create it.

- Abraham Lincoln, 16th President of the United States, 1809-1865

Future Light

Light tomorrow with today.

- Elizabeth Barrett Browning, English Poet, 1806-1861

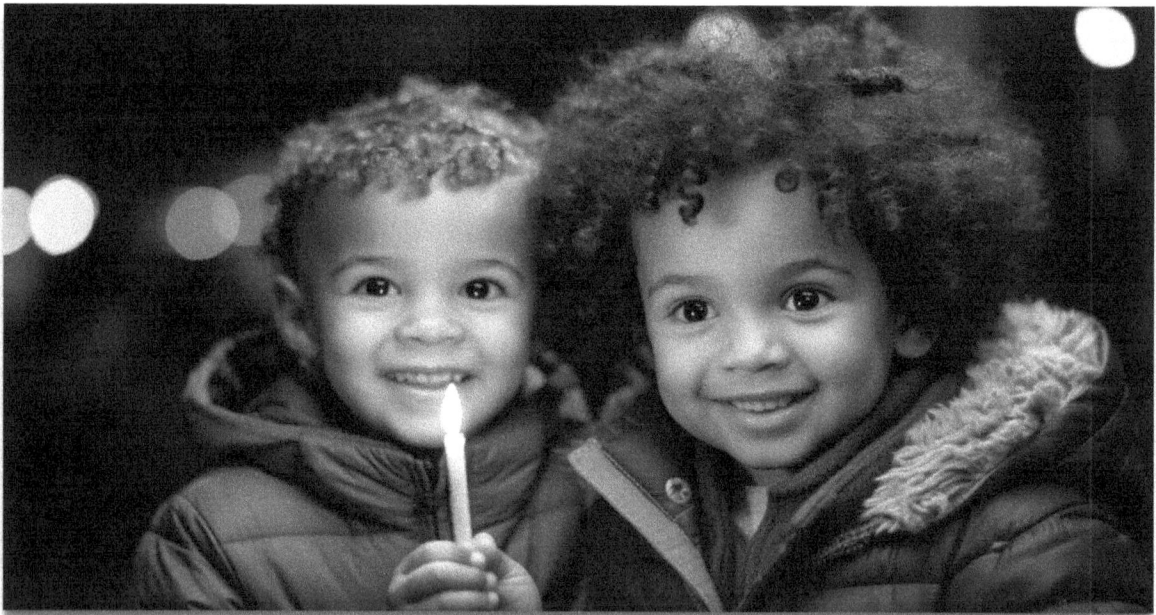

G

Generalizing Joke

All generalizing is false.

- Richie's Great Big Chicago Joke Book

Genius and Simplicity

The definition of genius is taking the complex and making it simple.

- Albert Einstein, German-born Theoretical Physicist, 1879-1955

Goals and Achievements

It always seems impossible until it's done.

- Nelson Mandela, President of South Africa and Freedom Fighter, 1918- 2013

Goals & Beliefs

Far away, there in the sunshine, are my highest aspirations. I may not reach them, but I can look up and see their beauty, believe in them, and try to follow where they lead.

- Louisa May Alcott, American Novelist, 1833-1888

God

What you seek is seeking you.

- Rumi, Islamic Poet and Mystic, 1207-1273

God and Mark Twain

A woman said to Mark Twain, "God must love you."

Twain later said, "Obviously, she doesn't realize that God and I are not getting along."

- Mark Twain in Eruption, Bernard Devoto, Published 1940

God & Nature

My Grandfather said he believed in God, but he spelled it N.A.T.U.R.E

- Penny Nichols, Tour guide at Yosemite CA in 1972

God, Gifts, and Work

God gives us wheat, but we must make the bread.

- Ukrainian Proverb

God is Lucky

You're lucky God, that you live so high in the sky; otherwise, people would break your windows.

- Russian Proverb

God Laughs

If you want to see God laugh, make a plan.

- Yiddish Proverb

God or Gods

Judaism has one God; Hinduism has three hundred million gods. Go figure!

- I heard a guy at Burning Man say this as he walked by. (He was painted blue from head to ankle.)

God's Sign Joke

If only God would give me some clear sign! Like making a large deposit in my name in a Swiss bank.

- Woody Allen, American Author, Filmmaker, Comedian, 1935-

Golden Rule

Don't do to anyone else what you wouldn't want done to you.

- Hebrew Golden Rule

Good Action

It's better to light a candle than curse the darkness.

- John F Kennedy, 35th President of the United States, 1917-1963

Good and Evil

Inside of me, there are two Wolves. One is mean and evil, and the other is good and understanding. They fight each other all the time. When asked which one wins, I answer, the one I feed the most.

- Sitting Bull, Lakota Chief and Medicine Man, 1831-1890

Good Fortune

Diligence is the mother of good fortune.

- German Proverb

Goodness

When you see someone's cloud, be their rainbow.

- Rose Garden, My Next-door Neighbor in San Diego Ca 1979

Government

The issue today is the same as it has been throughout all history, whether man shall be allowed to govern himself or be ruled by a small elite.

- Thomas Jefferson, 3rd President of the United States, 1743-1826

Grandfather's Walk

My grandfather always said, "A good walk in the hills is better for the spirit than church-goin." I agree with him.

- James McNeel, Tour Guide Zion National Park Utah, 1974

Grandparents

A grandparent is a little bit parent, a little bit teacher, and a little bit best friend.

- Janice Powers Gardening Aficionado, 1957-

Grandparents on Call

If nothing is going well, call your grandma.

- Miriam Friman, Purse and Wallet Saleswoman, Los Angeles CA 1916- 2007

Grief & Love

Grief is the price we pay for love.

- Queen Elizabeth the 2nd, Queen of the United Kingdom, 1926-2022

Grief That is Silent

There is no grief like the grief that does not speak.

- Henry Wadsworth Longfellow, American Poet, 1807-1882

Giving of Yourself

I do not give lengthy lectures or a little charity. When I give, I give myself.

- Walt Whitman, American Poet, 1819-1892

Growing Miracles

From a small seed, a mighty oak tree may grow.

- Aeschylus, Greek Playwright and Soldier, 524-456 BCE

Growing Up Always

You must do the things you think you cannot do.

- Eleanor Roosevelt, First Lady of the U.S. between 1944 and 1945, 1884-1962

Growing: Then or Now

The best time to plant a tree was 20 years ago. The second-best time is now.

- Chinese Proverb

H

Habit

You are what you repeatedly do.

- Aristotle, Greek Philosopher, 384-322 BCE

Habits

The second half of a man's life is made up of nothing but the habits he has acquired during the first half.

- Fyodor Dostoevsky, Russian Novelist, 1821-1881

Habits are like a Dry Ditch

In a ditch where water has flowed, it will flow again. So, be careful.

- Afghan Proverb

Habits Breaking

It is easier to prevent bad habits than to break them.

- Ben Franklin, Inventor, Printer, and Political Philosopher, 1706-1790

Happiness: Outside or Inside

Happiness is your nature. It is not wrong to desire it.

What is wrong is seeking it outside when it is inside.

- Ramana Maharshi, Hindu Sage, 1878-1950

Happiness When they Leave

Some cause happiness wherever they go, others whenever they go.

- Oscar Wilde, Irish Playwright and Poet, 1854-1900

Happiness & Unhappiness

The greatest happiness is to know the source of unhappiness.

- Fyodor Dostoevsky, Russian Novelist, 1821-1881

Happiness for Leo Tolstoy

Rest, nature, books, music…such is my idea of happiness.

- Leo Tolstoy, Russian Author, 1828-1910

Happiness Inside

Why are you so enchanted by this world when a gold mine lies within you?

- Rumi, Islamic Poet and Mystic, 1207-1273

Happiness: Self and Others

A sure way for one to lift oneself up is by helping to lift someone else.

- Booker T. Washington, Civil Rights Activist and Educator, 1856-1915

Happiness Takes Work

Every person is the blacksmith of their own happiness.

- Danish Proverb

Happiness with Nature

One of the first conditions of happiness is that the link between Man and Nature shall not be broken.

- Leo Tolstoy, Russian Author, 1828-1910

Hate and Love

Spend your time supporting what you love instead of knocking down what you oppose..

- Cornelis Willem Opzoomer, Dutch Lawyer and Philosopher, 1821-1892

Hating and Understanding

Folks never understand the folks they hate.

- James Russell Lowell, American poet, 1819-1891

Hat Joke

Q. What did one hat say to the other?

A. "You stay here! I'm going on a head."

- Richie's Great Big Chicago Joke Book

Healing & Nature

The art of medicine consists in amusing the patient while nature cures the disease.

- Voltaire, French Author and Philosopher, 1694-1778

Healing, Nature, and Nurses

Nature alone cures. What nursing has to do ... is to put the patient in the best condition for nature to act upon him.

- Florence Nightingale, *Mother of Modern Nursing, 1820-1910*

Health Gardeners

Your body is your garden. Your will is your gardener.

- Portuguese Saying

Health is Wealth

It is health that is real wealth, not money.

- Mahatma Gandhi, Nonviolent Anti Colonialist, Politician, 1869-1948

Health Joke

The only way to keep your health is to eat what you don't want to eat, drink what you don't want to drink, and do what you'd rather not.

- Mark Twain, American Author, 1835-1910

Health, Wealth, and Wisdom

Early to bed and early to rise, makes a man healthy, wealthy, and wise.

- Ben Franklin, Inventor, Printer, and Political Philosopher, 1706-1790

Health and Prevention

It is better to prevent than to cure.

- Peruvian Saying

Heart Opening

I believe much trouble and blood would be saved if we opened our hearts more.

- Chief Joseph, Nez Perce Chief, 1840-1904

Heartbreak

God is closest to those with broken hearts.

- Jewish Proverb

Heartbreak and Healing

The wound is the place where the light enters you.

- Rumi, Islamic Poet and Mystic, 1207-1273

Heaven and Hell

I don't want to go to heaven. None of my friends are there.

- Oscar Wilde, Irish Playwright and Poet, 1854-1900

Help Others

If you want happiness for 10 years, inherit some money. If you want happiness for a lifetime, help someone else to succeed.

- Confucius, Chinese Philosopher, 551 - 479 BCE

Helping Helps You

Those people who bring sunshine to others cannot keep it from themselves.

- James Barrie, Scottish Novelist and Playwright, Author of *Peter Pan*, 1860-1937

Helping Humanity

The desire that guides me in all I do, is the desire to harness the forces of nature to the service of mankind.

- Nikola Tesla, Austrian/American Inventor and Futurist, 1856-1943

Helping or Hurting

Whenever your life touches mine, you make me stronger or weaker.....there is no escape. People either drag each other down or lift them up.

- Booker T. Washington, Civil Rights Activist and Educator, 1856-1915

Helping Like a Light

Be a lamp, or a lifeboat, or a ladder. Help someone's soul heal. Walk out of your house like a shepherd.

- Rumi, Islamic Poet and Mystic, 1207-1273

Helping Others, Helping Yourself

If you help others, you will be helped, perhaps tomorrow, perhaps in one hundred years, but you will be helped.

- George Gurdjieff, Armenian/Greek Philosopher and Mystic, 1866-1949

Hero of Ourselves

The person who can destroy a thousand enemies is a minor hero compared to the person who overcomes himself.

- Rumi, Islamic Poet and Mystic, 1207-1273

Heroes After the War

Many heroes appear after the war.

- Romanian Proverb

Hippo Joke

Q: What's the difference between a Hippo and a Zippo?

A: One is really heavy, and the other is a little lighter.

- Richie's Great Big Chicago Joke Book

History Backwards and Forwards

The farther back in history that you look, the farther forward into the future you are likely to see.

- Mary Astell, English Author and Philosopher, 1666 -1731

History Education

Those who fail to learn from history are doomed to repeat it.

- George Santayanan, Spanish-American Philosopher, 1863-1952

History in High School Joke

Those of us who fail to learn history... are doomed to repeat it, in summer school.

- Hellen Wheels, Springfield High, Oregon, Class of 1964

History is a Fable

What is history but a fable agreed upon.

- Napoleon Bonaparte, French Emperor and Military Commander, 1769-1821

History and Nationalism

History is a threat to nationalism.

- F. H. Bradley, *British Philosopher, 1846 –1924*

History is Truthful?

History would be a wonderful thing – if it were only true.

- Leo Tolstoy, Russian Author, 1828-191

History Joke

Q. Why were the early days of history called the Dark Ages?

A. Because there were so many knights.

- Richie's Great Big Chicago Joke Book

Holiday Joke

I need a six-month holiday twice a year.

- An Egyptian man sitting on a park bench in Paris said this to me.

Home

We can't really appreciate home until we leave it.

- Morrie Chroman, L and M Plumbing, Los Angeles CA., 1926-2007

Honest or Not

To believe that everyone is honest is folly; but to believe that no one is honest is worse.

- John Quincy Adams, 6th President of United States, 1767-1848

Hope Alone

He who lives on hope, dies of starvation.

- Turkish Proverb

Hope and the Heart

If it was not for hope, the heart would break.

- Greek Proverb

Hope, but ....

Hope for miracles, but don't rely on them.

- Yiddish Proverb

Hopeless Teapot

I feel as hopeless as a chocolate teapot.

- Irish Expression

Horse Joke

Q. *Why didn't the pony talk?*

A. *Because it was a little hoarse.*

- Richie's Great Big Chicago Joke Book

Housework Joke

Housework doesn't make sense. You make your bed, you empty the trash, you put away your clothes, and three months later, it needs to be done all over again.

- Noah Zark, Storyteller at the Renaissance Faire, Agoura CA. 1973

Human Extremes

I am fascinated by the extremes of the human condition.

- Oscar Wilde, Irish Playwright and Poet, 1854-1900

Human Relations

Bring more presence, patience, humility, and humor to the conversation.

- Rosalind Annenberg, Award Winning Addiction Educator, Los Angeles, CA

Humans and Bicycles

Every time I see an adult on a bicycle, I no longer despair for the future of the human race.

- H. G. Wells, English Author, 1866-1946

Humans are Not Aliens

Nothing that is human is alien to me.

- Publius Terentius Afer, Roman Playwright, 185-159 BCE

Humiliation Doesn't Teach

Humiliation is a poor teacher.

- H. G. Wells, English Author, 1866-1946

Humility is the Gate

Only a person who has passed through the gate of humility can ascend to the heights of the spirit.

- Rudolph Steiner, Austrian Educator and Architect, 1861-1925

Humor and Brevity

Brevity is the soul of wit.

- William Shakespeare, English Playwright, 1564-1616

Humor and the Gods

Even the Gods love jokes.

- Plato, Greek Philosopher, 447-327 BCE

Humor & Truth

My way of joking is to tell the truth. It's the funniest joke in the world.

- George Bernard Shaw, Irish Playwright, 1856-1950

Humor is a Blessing

Humor is mankind's greatest blessing.

- Mark Twain, American Author, 1835-1910

Humor Saves Us

Humor is the great thing, the saving thing. The minute it crops up, all our irritations and resentments slip away, and a sunny spirit takes their place.

- Mark Twain, American Author, 1835-1910

Hunger & Anger

A hungry man is an angry man.

- English Proverb

Hunger as a Seasoning.

Hunger is the best seasoning.

- Mexican Saying

I

Ideas and Change

First, they will ignore you, then they will laugh at you, then they will fight you, and then you win.

- Mahatma Gandhi, Nonviolent Anti Colonialist, Politician, 1869-1948

Ideas vs Armies

No army can withstand the strength of an idea whose time has come.

- Victor Hugo, French Author,1802-1885

Idiots and Congress

Suppose you were an idiot, and suppose you were a member of Congress, but I repeat myself.

- Mark Twain, American Author, 1835-1910

Ignorance About Ourselves

The first reason for people's inner slavery is, above all, our ignorance of ourselves.

- George Gurdjieff, Armenian/Greek Philosopher and Mystic, 1866-1949

Ignorance and Apathy Joke

Q. Do you know the difference between ignorance and apathy?

A. I don't know, and I don't care.

- Richie's Great Big Chicago Joke Book

Ignorance in Crowds

A wise man makes his own decisions; the ignorant man goes with the crowd.

- Chinese Proverb

Illusions and Nothingness Joke

What if everything is an illusion and nothing exists? In that case, I definitely overpaid for my carpet.

- Woody Allen, American Author, Filmmaker, Comedian, 1935-

Imagination & Knowledge

Imagination is more important than knowledge.

- Albert Einstein, German-born Theoretical Physicist, 1879-1955

Imagined & Proven

What is now proved was once only imagined.

- William Blake, English Poet and Printmaker, 1757-1827

Immaturity Joke

Basically, my wife was immature. I'd be at home in the bath, and she'd come in and sink my boats.

- Woody Allen, American Film Maker, Author, Comedian 1935

Impossible Things

Sometimes I've believed as many as six impossible things before breakfast.

- Lewis Carroll, English Author, 1832-1898

Impossible Things 2

Alice: This is impossible.

The Mad Hatter: Only if you believe it is.

- Lewis Carroll, English Author, 1832-1898

Indifferencc to Politics

The price good men pay for indifference to politics is to be ruled by evil men.

- Plato, Greek Philosopher, 447-327 BCE

Individual and the Tribe

The individual has always had to struggle to keep from being overwhelmed by the tribe. If you try it, you will be lonely often, and sometimes frightened. But no price is too high to pay for the privilege of owning yourself.

- Rudyard Kipling, *English Author and Poet, 1865-1936*

Inevitable

What goes around comes around.

- French Saying

Infinite

Two things are infinite: the universe and human stupidity, and I'm not sure about the universe.

- Albert Einstein, German-born Theoretical Physicist, 1879-1955

Influence Over Others

Any time you think you have influence, try ordering around someone else's dog.

- Will Rogers, American Humorist, 1879-1935

Information Worth Knowing

The public has an insatiable curiosity to know everything except what is worth knowing.

- Oscar Wilde, Irish Playwright and Poet, 1854-1900

Inner Light

Your inner light grows when you water it with silence and concentration.

- Found in the Egyptian Temple of Luxor

Insect Joke

A dung beetle walks into a bar and says, "Excuse me, is this stool taken?"

- Richie's Great Big Chicago Joke Book

Inspiration: Gutters and Star

We are all in the gutter, but some of us are looking at the stars.

- Oscar Wilde, Irish Playwright and Poet, 1854-1900

Inspiration While Working

Don't wait for inspiration. It comes while one is working.

- Henri Matisse, French Artist, 1869-1954

Insult: Hello and Goodbye

I like your approach. Now I'd like to see your departure.

- Brian Snyder, Comedian Nevada County California, 1978-

Insult: What's Your Problem

I don't know what your problem is, but I'll bet it's hard to pronounce.

- I heard a guy say this at Meat and Greet Burgers in Newnan, GA.

Insult: Stay there

Someday you'll travel to far off lands, and I really hope you'll stay there.

- Terry Acci, Swimming Instructor at "Hawaiian Swim School", Los Angeles California

Intelligence?

Each generation imagines itself to be more intelligent than the one that went before it and wiser than the one that comes after it.

- George Orwell, English Novelist and Journalist, 1903-1950

Intelligence Joke

Q. What do you call a monster with a high IQ?

A. Frank-Einstein.

- Richie's Great Big Chicago Joke Book

Irish Joke

Q. Which country's capital has the fastest-growing population?

A. Ireland. Every day it's Dublin.

- Richie's Great Big Chicago Joke Book

Irony or Argument

At a time like this, scorching irony, not a convincing argument, is needed.

- Frederick Douglass, African American Social Reformer, Statesman, 1818-1895

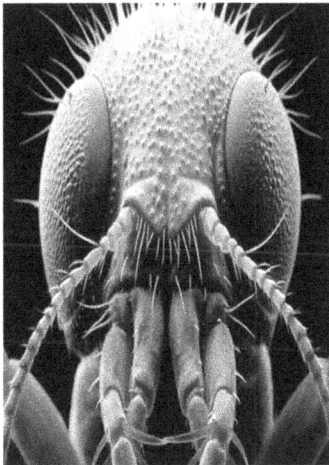

Irritating

Flea

A flea can trouble a lion more than a lion can trouble a flea.

- African Proverb

J

Jealousy Itches

The torment of jealousy is like a grain of sand in the eye.

- Chinese Proverb

Jealousy Joke

My girlfriend gets jealous when I go grocery shopping.

She says there's always a cashier checking me out.

- I heard this on a KVMR Radio comedy show, Nevada City CA, 2023

Jokes That Hurt

Jokes that hurt other people are not jokes.

- Miguel de Cervantes, Spanish Author, 1547-1616

Judgement Concerning Friends

Don't make friends with an elephant keeper if you don't have room for an elephant.

- Indian Proverb

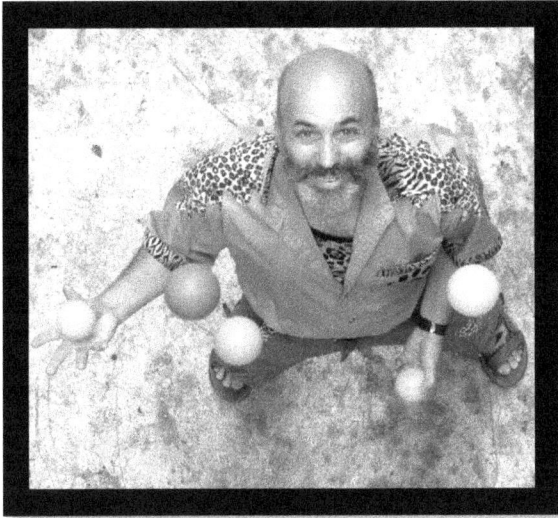

Juggling and Disease

Many diseases come from anxiety. Juggling helps us relax. It is an ancient form of therapy that has helped many fools to live long, fulfilling lives.

- Izzi Tooinsky, King of Hotdogastan, 1929-

Juggling For Happiness

Almost nothing can consistently make me feel so vital, so happy, and so alive, year after year, as juggling.

- Izzi Tooinsky, King of Hotdogastan, 1929-

Jungle Joke

Q. Why can't you play poker in the jungle?

A. Too many cheetahs!

- Richie's Great Big Chicago Joke Book

Junk Food

Don't fool yourself into thinking there is junk food. There is food, and there is junk. Make your choice.

- Leroy Johnson, Owned a fruit truck near my home in Inglewood CA in the 1970's

K

Kidnapping Joke

Q. Did you hear about the kidnapping at school?

A. It's ok. He woke up.

- Richie's Great Big Chicago Joke Book

Kindness

Be kind, for everyone you meet is fighting a hard battle.

- Socrates, Greek Philosopher, 469-399 BCE

Kindness, Even Little Bits Matter

No act of kindness, no matter how small, is ever wasted.

- Aesop, Greek Slave and Storyteller, 620-556 BCE

Kind Words

Kind words do not cost you much, but they accomplish much.

- Blaise Pascal, French Mathematician, Inventor, and Philosopher, 1623-1662

Kings and Soldiers

The soldiers fight, and the kings are called the heroes.

- Turkish Proverb

Kiss Affect

The sound of a kiss is not as loud as a cannon, but its echo lasts a great deal longer.

- Oliver Wendell Holmes Jr., American Judge, 1841-1935

Knowledge and Ignorance

Real knowledge is to know the extent of one's ignorance.

- Confucius, Chinese Philosopher, 551 - 479 BCE

Knowledge Explained to Grandma

You never truly understand something until you can explain it to your grandmother.

- Albert Einstein, German-born Theoretical Physicist, 1879-195

Knowledge Inside or Outside

So long as God seems to be outside and far away, there is ignorance. But when God is realized within, that is true knowledge.

- Rama Krishna, Indian Mystic and Teacher, 1836-1886

L

Laughter is Catching

There is nothing in the world so irresistibly contagious as laughter.

- Charles Dickens, English Author, 1812-1870

Laughter is Warm

Laughter is the sun that drives winter from the human face.

- Victor Hugo, French Author, 1802-1885

Laughter Lost

Man, when you lose your laugh, you lose your footing.

- Ken Kesey, American novelist, 1935-2001

Laughter: Young and Old

You don't stop laughing when you grow old. You grow old when you stop laughing.

- George Bernard Shaw, Irish Playwright, 1856-1950

Laws for Good and Bad People

Good people do not need laws to tell them to act responsibly, while bad people will find a way around the laws.

- Plato, Greek Philosopher, 447-327 BCE

Laws like Spider Webs

Laws are spider webs through which the big flies pass, and the little ones get caught.

- Honore de Balzac, French Novelist and Playwright, 1799-1850

Lawyers and Simple Folk

A peasant between two lawyers is like a fish between two cats.

- Catalonian Proverb

Leadership Leaves a Trail

Do not go where the path may lead, go instead where there is no path and leave a trail.

- Ralph Waldo Emerson, American Philosopher, 1803-1882

Leading Gently

A leader is best when people barely know he exists.

- Lao Tzu, Legendary Chinese Philosopher, 604-531 BCE

Leading Sheep or Lions

An army of sheep led by a lion would defeat an army of lions led by a sheep.

- Arabic Proverb

Leadership Qualities

If your actions inspire others to dream more, learn more, do more, and become more, you are a leader.

- John Quincy Adams, 6th President of U.S.A, 1767-1848

Learning & Falling

Falling down is part of learning how to walk.

- *Kazakh Proverb*

Learning To Fish

Give a man a fish and you feed him for a day......
Teach a man to fish and you feed him for a lifetime.

- Maimonides, Spanish/Egyptian Talmudist, Physician, Philosopher, 1138-1204

Learning To Fish Joke

Give a man a fish and you feed him for a day……

Teach a man to fish and you can get rid of him for the whole weekend.

- Richie's Great Big Chicago Joke Book

Learning To Ride

If you want to be a good rider, saddle the worst horse; for if you can tame that one, you can tame them all.

- Socrates, Greek Philosopher, 469-399 BCE

Lies; Big and Small

The bigger the lie, the more people will believe it.

- Joseph Goebbels, Propagandist of the Nazi regime, 1887-1945

Lies Travel Fast

A lie can travel halfway around the world while the truth is putting on its shoes.

- Mark Twain, American Author, 1835-1910

Life and Death

Life is so good, why would we assume that death would be otherwise?

- Rabindranath Tagore, Indian Playwright and Poet, 1861-1941

Life and Death 2

Any moment might be our last. Everything is more beautiful because we're doomed.

- Homer, Greek Poet, 800 BCE

Life & Idiots

Out Out Brief Candle!

Life is but a walking shadow,

a poor player that struts and frets his hour upon the stage and then is heard no more.

It is a tale told by an idiot, full of sound and fury, signifying nothing.

- William Shakespeare, English Playwright 1564-1616

Life is......

Life is a dream for the wise, a game for the fool, a comedy for the rich, and a tragedy for the poor.

- Sholem Aleichem, Russian/American Yiddish Author, 1859-1916

Life Unexamined

The unexamined life is not worth living.

- Socrates, Greek Philosopher, 469-399 BCE

Light Year Joke

Q. What's a Light Year?

A. It's like a regular year, just less calories.

- Richie's Great Big Chicago Joke Book

Lincoln's Simple Religion

When I do good, I feel good. When I do bad, I feel bad. That's my religion.

- Abraham Lincoln, 16thPresident of the United States, 1809-1865

Living Well

When giving, be kind. When speaking, be truthful. When ruling, be just. When working, be one-pointed. When acting, remember – timing is everything.

- Lao Tzu, Legendary Chinese Philosopher, 604-531 BCE

Loneliness is Preferable

In a choice between bad company and loneliness — the second is preferable.

- Spanish Parable

Loneliness With Yourself

The worse loneliness is not to be comfortable with yourself.

- Mark Twain, American Author, 1835-1910

Loss and the Value of Things

Mostly it is loss that teaches us about the value of things.

- Arthur Schopenhauer, German Philosopher, 1788-1860

Love All

Love all, trust a few, do wrong to none.

- William Shakespeare, English Playwright 1564-1616

Love & Courage

Because of great love, one is courageous.

- Lao Tzu, Legendary Chinese Philosopher, 604-531 BCE

Love and Doubt

I was in love; she was in doubt.

- Noah Zark, Storyteller at Renaissance Faire, Agoura CA, 1973

Love and Tenderness

Love is like a baby: it needs to be treated tenderly.

- Congolese Saying

Love in Childhood

Little Red Riding Hood was my first love. I felt that if I could have married Little Red Riding Hood, I would have known perfect bliss.

- Charles Dickens, English Author, 1812-1870

Love Is Not Smooth!

The course of true love never did run smooth.

- William Shakespeare, English Playwright 1564-1616

Love Makes Way

Love starts when we push aside our own ego and make room for somebody else.

- Rudolph Steiner, Austrian Educator and Social Reformer, 1861-1925

Love Shown

They do not love that do not show their love.

- William Shakespeare, English Playwright 1564-1616

Love Shows You the Way

If you've got love in your heart, whatever you do from that moment out is likely to be right. If you've got that one true note ringing inside you, then whatever you do is going to be OK.

- Ken Kesey, American novelist, 1935-2001

Love Understood

Life's greatest happiness is to fully understand that we are loved.

- Victor Hugo, French Author,1802-1885

Love Your Life

Love your life, perfect your life, and beautify all things in your life.

- Tecumseh, Shawnee Chief and Warrior, 1768-1813

Loved & Lost

Tis better to have loved and lost than never to have loved at all.

- Alfred Lord Tennyson, British Poet, 1809-1892

Loving Others

Those who are hardest to love need it the most.

- Socrates, Greek Philosopher, 469-399 BCE

M

Madness of Greatness

No great mind has ever existed without a touch of madness.

- Aristotle, Greek Philosopher, 384-322 BCE

Marriage and Luck

Marriage is a little bit like buying melons; you need a little luck.

- Spanish Proverb

Marriage and Mothers

Women beware! Never, ever marry a man who hated his mother.

- Grace Jumba, my psychology professor at the International University of Africa, Nairobi Kenya, 1978

Marriage: Good and Bad

By all means, marry. If you get a good wife, you'll become happy. If you get a bad one, you'll become a philosopher.

- Socrates, Greek Philosopher, 469-399 BCE

Marriage Joke

Frequently I wake up grumpy. But just as often, I let her sleep.

- A man said this to me as we traveled on the train from Sydney to Newcastle Australia, 2002

Marriage, Loss, Revenge

When a man steals your wife, there is no better revenge than to let him keep her.

- Sacha Guitry, French Actor and Director, 1885-1957

Marriage Shines Forth

There is nothing more admirable than when two people, who see eye to eye, keep house as man and wife, confounding their enemies and delighting their friends.

- Homer, Greek Poet, 8th Century BCE

Marriage, The Eye Opener

Love is blind, but marriage is a real eye-opener.

- My uncle Unko would whisper this to all the young men at our family weddings.

Married Men and Inventions

I do not think you can name many great inventions that have been made by married men.

- Nikola Tesla, Austrian/American Inventor and Futurist, 1856-1943

$$\frac{1}{2}$$

← numerator

← ?

← denominator

Math Joke

In a fraction, there is a fine line between a numerator and a denominator.

- Richie's Great Big Chicago Joke Book

Math Joke 2

Q. How do you make 7 even?

A. Take away the s.

- Richie's Great Big Chicago Joke Book

Maturity & Work

Maturing is the ability to work on something until it's done.

- **Confucius,** Chinese Philosopher, 551 - 479 BCE

Meaning and the Planting of Trees

The one who plants trees, knowing that he will never sit in their shade, has at least started to understand the meaning of life.

- Rabindranath Tagore, Indian Playwright and Poet, 1861-1941

Meaning of Life

The sole meaning of life is to serve humanity.

- Leo Tolstoy, Russian Author, 1828-1910

Medical Joke

Q. If a basketball player gets athlete's feet, what does an astronaut get?

A. Missile Toe!

- Richie's Great Big Chicago Joke Book

Medicine or Not

The greatest medicine of all is teaching people how not to need it.

- Hippocrates, Greek Physician, 460-370 BCE

Meditate and Listen

There is a voice that doesn't use words. Listen.

- Rumi, Islamic Poet and Mystic, 1207-1273

Meditation and Hearing

The quieter you become, the more you are able to hear.

- Rumi, Islamic Poet and Mystic, 1207-1273

Meditation and Rest

In short, give up doer and deed. Rest in "Nondoing."

- Tulku Urgyen Rinpoche, Tibetan Meditation Teacher, 1920-1996

Memory Joke

I never forget a face, but in your case, I'll be glad to make an exception.

- Groucho Marx, American Comedian, 1890-1977

Men and Women

Nothing is so necessary for a young man as the company of intelligent women.

- Leo Tolstoy, Russian Author, 1828-1910

Men Standing Tall

No man stands taller than when he stoops to help a child.

- Abraham Lincoln, 16th President of the United States, 1809-1865

Men's Riches

Children are a poor man's riches.

- English Proverb

Mental Health All over the World

Across the world, more and more people are realizing that mental illness is a disease that should be treated just like any other illness. Seeking help for mental health issues is an important step towards achieving lasting healing and happiness.

- Ministry of Health in Hotdogastan

Mental Illness in History

(People with mental illnesses are), confined within cages, closets, cellars, stalls, pens; chained, naked, beaten with rods; and lashed into obedience.

- Dorothea Dix, Mental Health Advocate, 1802-1887

Minds and Mouths

Why is it that people with the narrowest minds seem to have the widest mouths?

- Lewis Carroll, English Author, 1832-1898

Miracles

The miracle is that everyone matters.

- Paulette Mahurin, My Cousin and well-known author of *The Seven Year Dress* and many other novels.

Misery Comes From….

All men's miseries derive from not being able to sit in a quiet room alone.

- Blaise Pascal, French Mathematician, Inventor, and Philosopher.1623-1662

Mistakes

Always leave a little room for a mistake.

- Chinese Saying

Mistakes Are Stepping Stones

Don't be afraid of mistakes. They are the stepping-stones that lead to future accomplishments.

- Baal Shem Tov, Jewish Mystic and Healer, 1668-1760

Mom

Did you know that Mom, written upside down, is Wow!

- First first-grader said this to me when I was performing in Lake Tahoe Nevada, 2022

Mom's Strawberry Joke

Q. Why did the little strawberry cry?

A. Its mom was in a jam.

- Richie's Great Big Chicago Joke Book

Money is like a Turtle and a Gazelle

Wealth comes like a turtle and runs away like a gazelle.

- Arabic Parable

Money Spent

Too many people spend money they haven't earned to buy things they don't want, to impress people they don't like.

- Will Rogers, American Humorist, 1879-1935

Money, Use It

Money is like an arm or leg - use it or lose it.

- Henry Ford, American Industrialist, 1863-1947

Mothers

God could not be everywhere, and therefore he made mothers.

- Rudyard Kipling, English Author, 1865-1936

Mothers 2

As is the mother, so is her daughter.

- Ezekiel 16:4

Mothers 3

Sometimes I open my mouth, and my mother comes out.

- Albert Einstein, German-born Theoretical Physicist, 1879-1955

Mothers 4

You wrestled a bear? Cool. I removed a splinter from a two-year-old's finger. I think we're even.

- Abby Chroman, Working Mom, Working Traveler, Youngest of my 12 Daughters.

Mothers and Troubles

My mother had a great deal of trouble with me, but I think she enjoyed it.

- Mark Twain, American Author, 1835-1910

Mothers in Bathrooms

You know you're a mom when you stop dreaming about winning the lottery and start imagining how great it would be to go to the bathroom alone.

- I overheard a woman say this at Nacho Average Tacos in Antioch, CA. 2020

Mountains Speak

Society speaks and all men listen, mountains speak, and wise men listen.

- John Muir, Father of the American National Parks, 1838-1914

Murder

It is forbidden to kill; therefore, all murderers are punished, unless they kill in large numbers and to the sound of trumpets.

- Voltaire, French Author and Philosopher, 1694-1778

Music

Where words fail, music speaks.

- Hans Christian Anderson, Danish author, 1805-1875

Music Joke

Two windmills are standing in a wind farm. One asks,

"What's your favorite kind of music?"

The other answers, "I'm a big metal fan."

- Richie's Great Big Chicago Joke Book

Music is a Language

Music is the universal language of mankind.

- Henry Wadsworth Longfellow, American Poet, 1807-188

Musical Silence

Silence is music to a wise man.

- Turkish Proverb

Mystery To Be Lived

Life is a mystery to be lived, not a problem to be solved.

- Søren Aabye Kierkegaard, Danish Theologian and Philosopher, 1813-1855

N

Name Joke

I'd like to name my kid a whole phrase. You know, something like "Ladies and Gentlemen". That'll be a cool name for a kid. "This is my son, Ladies and Gentlemen!" Then, when he gets out of hand, I get to go, "Ladies and Gentlemen, please be quiet!"

- Louis C.K., American Comedian, 1967-

Nationality

Every nationality teaches its own exceptionalism.

- Sherman Oaks, High School History Teacher, Omaha Nebraska

Nationality 2

Our true nationality is mankind.

- H. G. Wells, English Author, 1866-1946

Nations

The greatness of a nation and its moral progress can be judged by the way its animals are treated.

- Mahatma Gandhi, Nonviolent Anti Colonialist, Politician, 1869-1948

Nations and Homes

The ruin of a nation begins in the homes of its people.

- Cornelis Willem Opzoomer, Dutch Lawyer and Philosopher, 1821-1892

Native American Prayer

Help me always to speak the truth quietly, to listen with an open mind when others speak, and to remember the peace that may be found in silence.

● Cherokee Prayer

Nature

When a man moves away from nature, his heart becomes hard.

● Lakota Teaching

Nature and Doctors

Nature itself is the best physician.

● Hippocrates, Greek Physician, 460-370 BCE

Nature is Medicine

I go to nature to be soothed and healed and to have my senses put in order.

● John Burroghs, American Author and Naturalist, 1832-1921

Nature Rejuvenates

Keep close to Nature's heart... Break clear away every once in a while and climb a mountain or spend a week in the woods. Wash your spirit clean.

- John Muir, Father of the American National Parks, 1838-1914

Nature's Medicine

Nature, time, and patience are the three great physicians.

- Bulgarian Proverb

Nature's Medicine 2

Thousands of tired, nerve-shaken, over-civilized people are beginning to find out that going to the mountains is going home; and that wildness is a necessity.

- John Muir, Father of the American National Parks, 1838-1914

Negative People

Don't walk away from negative people – run!

- Mark Twain, American Author, 1835-1910

Negative People 2

Let go of negative people. They only show up to share complaints, problems, disastrous stories, fear, and judgment of others. If somebody is looking for a bin to throw all their trash into, make sure it's not in your mind.

- Dalai Lama, Tibetan Spiritual Teacher, 1935-

Negativity; Quiet Down

The person who says it cannot be done should not interrupt the person who is doing it.

- Chinese Proverb

Neighbors and Houses

Anyone can buy a good house, but good neighbors are priceless.

- Vietnamese Proverb

Neighbors and the Devil

People have discovered that they can fool the devil, but they can't fool the neighbors.

- Francis Bacon, English Philosopher and Statesman, 1561-1626

Neighbors & Tubas

Love your neighbor, even if he plays the tuba.

- Yiddish Proverb

Nonsense

I love to talk about nothing. It's the only thing I know anything about.

- Oscar Wilde, Irish Playwright and Poet, 1854-1900

Non-violence and Humiliation

The first principle of non-violent action is that of noncooperation with everything humiliating.

- Mahatma Gandhi, Nonviolent Anti Colonialist, Politician, 1869-1948

Normal

Normality is a paved road: It's comfortable to walk, but no flowers grow on it.

- Vincent van Gogh, Dutch Painter, 1853-1890

Number Joke

Q. What did the zero say to the 8?

A. "Hey, nice belt."

- Richie's Great Big Chicago Joke Book

Numbers Joke 2

There are three kinds of people; those who can count and those who can't.

- Richie's Great Big Chicago Joke Book

Nursing and Heroes

Save one life and you're a hero. Save a hundred lives and you're a nurse.

- Well known anonymous phrase honoring all nurses.

Nursing is an Art

Nursing is an art: It requires an exclusive devotion as hard in preparation as any painter or sculptor's work.

- Florence Nightingale, Mother of Modern Nursing, 1820-1910

Nursing Joy

When you are a nurse, you know that every day you will touch a life, or a life will touch yours.

- Ann Onymous, Official Feet Warmer for Louise, Duchess of Fife, 1867-1931

O

Obstacles & Goals

Obstacles are those frightful things you see when you take your eyes off your goals.

- Henry Ford, American Industrialist, 1863-1947

Old Age Joke

Q. *Which underwear brand do senior citizens love best?*

A. *Depends.*

- Richie's Great Big Chicago Joke Book

Old Age

Cherish youth but trust old age.

- Pueblo Teaching

Old Age with Sweetness

The older the violin, the sweeter the music.

- Ukrainian Proverb

Old Age - Young Mind

Anyone who stops learning is old, whether at twenty or eighty. Anyone who keeps learning stays young. The greatest thing in life is to keep your mind young.

- Henry Ford, American Industrialist, 1863-1947

Oneness

Oneness means a feeling, a knowing, that we are not separate from all living things. That we exist on a wonderous universal web, created and sustained by a consciousness beyond our ability to comprehend.

- Iona Frisbee, My Cousin's Grandma's Small Engine Mechanic, Dinosaur Colorado

Oneness Joke

Q. What did the Zen Monk say to the hot dog vendor?

A. Make me one with everything!

- Richie's Great Big Chicago Joke Book

Onion Joke

A lot of people cry when they cut an onion. The trick is not to form an emotional bond.

- Richie's Great Big Chicago Joke Book

Opportunity & Chaos

In the midst of chaos, there is also opportunity.

- Sun Tzu, Ancient Chinese military general, around 256

Optimism and Pessimism

Both optimists and pessimists contribute to society. The optimist invents the airplane, the pessimist the parachute.

- George Bernard Shaw, Irish Playwright, 1856-1950

Opportunity's Door

The door of opportunity will not open unless you do some pushing.

- Terry Mahurin, All Around Great Guy

Originality

Plant a garden in which strange plants grow and mysteries bloom.

- Ken Kesey, American novelist, 1935-2001

P

Pain & Love

Where there is great love, sooner or later there will be great pain.

- Italian Proverb

Pain of the Mind

Pain of the mind is worse than pain of the body.

- Latin Proverb

Paradox: Good and Bad

I am as bad us the worst, but thank God, I am as good as the best.

- Walt Whitman, American Poet, 1819-1892

Parents

The best way to get your children's attention is to relax and look comfortable.

- Charleen Mortez, Nanny Extraordinary, Santa Barbara California

Parents and Children

Parents and children teach one another.

- Japanese Proverb

Parents and Zippers

The true test of patience is watching your 8-year-old try to zip their coat themselves when you are running late.

- Thea Chroman, Working Mom, Eldest of my 12 daughters.

Parent's Complaint

When a parent complains, "My child has become cruel and hard. What should I do?" The answer is, "Love them more than ever."

- Baal Shem Tov, Jewish Mystic and Healer, 1668-1760

Parents Joke

I can trace my genealogy all the way back to my parents.

- Rachael James Snyder, Author, Editor and Chief of Atlas Obscura, 1976-

Past Regrets

Regretting the past is like chasing after the wind.

- Russian Proverb

Patience is Sweet

Patience is bitter, but its fruit is sweet.

- Aristotle, Greek Philosopher, 384-322 BCE

Patriotism

Patriotism is, fundamentally, a conviction that a particular country is the best in the world because you were born in it.

- George Bernard Shaw, Irish Playwright, 1856-1950

Patriotism 2

Patriotism is the last refuge of a scoundrel.

- Dr Samuel Johnson, English Author and Critic, 1709-1784

Payment in Advance

The musician who is paid in advance does not play as well.

- Nicaraguan Proverb

Peace and Beans

Better to eat beans in peace than to eat meat in distress.

- Guatemalan Proverb

Peace & Madness

It is madness for a sheep to talk of peace with a wolf.

- French Proverb

Peace and Truth

Be quiet in your mind, quiet in your senses, and also quiet in your body. Then, when all these are quiet, don't do anything. In that state, truth will reveal itself to you.

- Kabir, Indian Mystic, 1440-1518

Peace is Not Cheap

Peace is costly but it is worth the expense.

- African Proverb

Peace Joke

The Man Who Created Autocorrect Has Died. May he restaurant In Peace.

- Richie's Great Big Chicago Joke Book

People Joke 2

Sometimes you meet someone, and from that very first moment, you know you want to spend your whole life without them.

- I overheard a woman at Starbucks, in Whynot Carolina, say this comment into her phone.

Perfection

Have no fear of perfection, you'll never achieve it.

- Marie Curie, Polish -French Physicist and Chemist, 1867-1934

Perseverance & Disturbances

The dogs may bark, but the caravan moves on.

- Arabic Parable

Perseverance: Over and Over

The greatest glory in living lies not in never falling, but in rising every time we fall.

- Nelson Mandela, President of South Africa and Freedom Fighter, 1918- 2013

Perseverance Secret

Perseverance is the secret of all triumphs.

- Victor Hugo, French Author,1802-1885

Persevere: Don't Stop!

It does not matter how slowly you go, as long as you do not stop.

- Confucius, Chinese Philosopher, 551 - 479 BCE

Persist Until One Day...

It always seems impossible until it is done.

- Nelson Mandela, President of South African and Freedom Fighter, 1918- 2013

Persistence Guarantees

Persistence guarantees that results are inevitable.

- Paramahansa Yogananda, Hindu Monk and Founder of Self Realization Fellowship, 1893-1952

Persistence is An Art

Starting is easy, persistence is an art.

- German Saying

Persistence Joke

If at first you don't succeed, maybe you should skip bungee jumping.

- Richie's Great Big Chicago Joke Book

Personal Power

The greater your real strength and power, the quieter it will be exercised.

- James Russell Lowell, American poet, 1819-1891

Perspective

You don't really see the world if you only look through your own window.

- Ukrainian Proverb

Perspective is Yours

A man sees in the world what he carries in his heart.

- Johann Wolfgang von Goethe, German Author, 1749-1832

Perspective of a Hammer

To a hammer, every problem looks like a nail.

- American Proverb

Pessimism and Optimism

There is no sadder sight than a young pessimist, except an old optimist.

- Mark Twain, American Author, 1835-1910

Pets For Presidents

Any man who does not like dogs ... does not deserve to be in the White House.

- Calvin Coolidge, 30th President of the United States of America, 1872-1933

Photographing Faces

There are no bad pictures; that's just how your face looks sometimes.

- Abraham Lincoln, 16th President of the United States, 1809-1865

Piano Joke

Q. *What do you get when you drop a piano down a mine shaft?*

A. *A flat miner.*

- Richie's Great Big Chicago Joke Book

Pilgrimage Inside

I felt in need of a great pilgrimage, so I sat still for three days, and God came to me.

- Kabir, Indian Mystic, 1440-1518

Pirate Joke

Q. What did the pirate say on his 80th birthday?

A. Aye Matie!

- Richie's Great Big Chicago Joke Book

Plans and Foolishness

Mix a little foolishness with your serious plans. It's lovely to be silly at the right moments.

- Horace, Roman Poet, 65-8 BCE

Plants Talk

All plants are our brothers and sisters. They talk to us, and if we listen, we can hear them.

- Arapaho Teaching

Plant Medicine

For every human illness, somewhere in the world, there exists a plant that is the cure.

- John Quincy Adams, 6th President of U.S.A, 1767-1848.

Planting Happiness

He who plants a garden, plants happiness.

- Ukrainian Proverb

Play and Aging

We don't stop playing because we grow old; we grow old because we stop playing.

- George Bernard Shaw, Irish Playwright, 1856-1950

Play & Juggling

Juggling and all creative play is a balance between spontaneity and discipline.

- Izzi Tooinsky, King of Hotdogastan, 1929-

Play and Screaming

Sometimes we scream when we play. In very few other activities is it okay to scream. It feels very good to scream every once in a while.

- Kate Duroux, French Musician, Juggler, Fool, 1947-

Play, and Understand the World

We should realize that children at play are not wasting time; their games should be seen as their way to understand the world.

- Michel de Montaigne, French Philosopher, 1513-1592

Play is Research

Play is the highest form of research.

- Albert Einstein, German-born Theoretical Physicist, 1879-1955

Play vs Conversation

You can discover more about a person in an hour of play than in a year of conversation.

- Plato, Greek Philosopher, 447-327 BCE

Playing Outdoors

Outdoor play is among the greatest gifts we can give our children. Adventurous and curious children are among the greatest gifts we can give our communities.

- Message on the back of a Chocolate Brownie Flavored Clif Bar.

Playing Rough

Rough play and horsing around have great value. They help our children become confident interpersonally and relaxed socially.

- Art Browning, Family Counselor, Fremantle Australia, 2004

Police Joke

Officer Asks Mike, "Why did you park here?"

Mike Answers, "The sign says, 'Fine for parking."

- Richie's Great Big Chicago Joke Book

Police Joke 2

An officer pulled me over, walked to my window and said "Papers."

I said, "Scissors. I win!" and drove off.

I guess he wants a rematch because he's been following me for about 30 minutes.

- Richie's Great Big Chicago Joke Book

Political Participation

One of the penalties of refusing to participate in politics is that you end up being governed by your inferiors.

- Plato, Greek Philosopher, 447-327 BCE

Politics and Negotiations

Let us never negotiate out of fear. But let us never fear to negotiate.

- John F Kennedy, 35th President of the United States, 1917-1963

Poverty and Crime

Poverty is the mother of crime.

- Marcus Aurelius, Roman emperor, 121-181.

Poverty Breeds Disrespect

Poverty is a noose that strangles humanity and breeds disrespect for God and man.

- Sioux Proverb

Poverty in the Bones

The chill of poverty never leaves your bones.

- George Bernard Shaw, Irish Playwright, 1856-1950

Poverty is Heavy

The heaviest thing in the world is an empty pocket.

- Turkish Proverb

Poverty Vow

I've taken an involuntary vow of poverty.

- Geoffrey Chaucer, English poet, author, 1340-1400

Power in the Eyes of the Beholder

Every rooster crows on its own dunghill.

- Arabic Proverb

Power Changes Hands

Every dog has its day.

- Portuguese Proverb

Power Test

Nearly all men can stand adversity, but if you want to test a man's character, give him power.

- Abraham Lincoln, 16th President of the United States, 1809-1865

Power Roars

Sometimes, the lion must roar so that the zebra remembers who's in charge.

- Kenyan Proverb

Prayer & Stomachs

A hungry stomach makes a short prayer.

- Paiute Proverb

Prejudices for Fools

Prejudices are what fools use for reason.

- Voltaire, French Author and Philosopher, 1694-1778

Presidential Grief

The four most miserable years of my life were my four years in the presidency.

- John Quincy Adams, 6th President of U.S.A, 1767-1848

Pressure Makes Diamonds

No pressure, no diamonds.

- Thomas Carlyle, Scottish Historian and Philosopher, 1795-1891

Pressure Sometimes is Necessary

If you can't handle the heat, get out of the kitchen.

- American Proverb

Prevention

An ounce of prevention is worth a pound of cure.

- Dutch Proverb

Pride

Pride comes before the fall.

- English Proverb

Pride and Disaster

Pride and excess bring disaster for man.

- *Xun Kuang*, Chinese Philosopher, 310-238 BCE

Pride & Humility

Pride is concerned with who is right. Humility is concerned with what is right.

- Pakistani Proverb

Primates Preoccupations

Sex, territory, and hierarchy are the main preoccupations of primates.

- Jerry Atric, my tour guide at the San Diego Wild Animal Park, 1983

Prison Joke

English Teacher: I want you to tell me the longest sentence you can think of.

Pupil: Life imprisonment!

- Richie's Great Big Chicago Joke Book

Problems and Blessings

Count your blessings, not your problems.

- Susan Chroman, Lifetime Friend and Sister.

Problems & Dreams

Don't be pushed by your problems. Be led by your dreams.

- Ralph Waldo Emerson, American Philosopher, 1803-1882

Procrastinate Tomorrow

Never put off till tomorrow what may be done the day after tomorrow just as well.

- Mark Twain, American Author, 1835-1910

Progress and Struggle

If there is no struggle, there is no progress.

- Frederick Douglass, African American Social Reformer, Statesman, 1818-1895

Promises

Where people are promising much, bring a small bag.

- Bosnian Proverb

Prophets and Fools

The complete fool is half a prophet.

- Yiddish Proverb

Proverbs are Short

A proverb is a short sentence based on long experience.

- Miguel de Cervantes, Spanish Author, 1547-1616

Proverbs in Conversation

Proverbs in conversation are torches in darkness.

- Venezuelan Prover

Proverbs of Quality

A country can be judged by the quality of its proverbs.

- German Proverb

Punishment Hungry

Distrust all in whom the impulse to punish is powerful.

- Fredrich Nietzsche, German Philosopher, 1844-1900

Purpose of Life

Your purpose in life is to find your purpose in life and to give your whole heart and soul to it.

- Gautama Buddha, Founder of Buddhism, 563 - 480 BCE

Purpose of Life 2

The purpose of life is not to simply exist, but to live fully and passionately.

- Baal Shem Tov, Jewish Mystic and Healer, 1668-1760

Q

Question Joke

A police officer saw a woman standing in the middle of a crowded street. He dodged a hundred cars and trucks, ran to her and panted, "Are you OK?" The woman answered, "Yes, but how do I get to the hospital?" The officer said, "Just keep standing there."

- Richie's Great Big Chicago Joke Book

Questions Are OK

Better to ask ten times than go astray once.

- Argentine Proverb

Quiet is Good

Never miss a good chance to shut up.

- Will Rogers, American Humorist, 1879-1935

R

Reacting Too Much!

Don't make a mountain out of a molehill.

- English Proverb

Reading for the Mind

Reading is to the mind what exercise is to the body.

- Joseph Addison, English Playwright, Poet, and Politician, 1672-1719

Reading Leaders

Today a reader; tomorrow a leader.

- Margaret Fuller, American Journalist and Women's Rights Advocate, 1810-1850

Reading One Book

Beware of the person of just one book.

- Thomas Aquinas, Italian Priest and Philosopher, 1225-1274

Reading People or Words

I can't read little things like letters. I read big things, like men.

- Sojourner Truth, American Abolitionist, Died 1883

Real Men and a Child's Trust

You are not a real man until you have earned the trust of a child.

- Pashtun Saying

Real to Me

I'm not strange, weird, off, nor crazy. My reality is just different from yours.

- Lewis Carroll, English Author, 1832-1898

Reason and Beyond

The supreme function of reason is to show man that some things are beyond reason.

- Blaise Pascal, French mathematician, Inventor, and Philosopher. 1623-1662

Rebellion

I believe that a little rebellion now and then is a good thing, and as necessary in the political world as storms in the physical world.

- Thomas Jefferson, 3ʳᵈ President of the United States, 1743-1826

Receiving and Giving

Our mind is enriched by what we receive, our heart by what we give.

- Victor Hugo, French Author, 1802-188

Red Hair

Red hair is God's way of giving humanity roses.

- Anita Perm, French Cosmetologist for Louie XVI, 1751- 1792

Re-Examine

Re-examine all that you have been told... dismiss that which insults your soul.

- Walt Whitman, American Poet, 1819-1892

Relationships

When I first saw you, I fell in love, and you smiled because you knew.

- William Shakespeare, English Playwright
  1564-1616

Relationships and Cats

No matter how much cats fight, there always seem to be plenty of kittens.

- Abraham Lincoln, 16th President of the United States, 1809-1865

Relationships & Love

To know that the other person is imperfect, but to love them anyways, that's what makes a good relationship.

- Paulette Mahurin, My Cousin and well-known author of *The Seven Year Dress* and many other novels.

Relationships and Your Cheeks

I don't want learning, or dignity, or respectability. I want this music, and this dawn, and the warmth of your cheek against mine.

- Rumi, Islamic Poet and Mystic, 1207-1273

Relationships with Loved Ones

All relationships are bumpy. Have patience. Develop relationship skills. It will be OK.

- Rosalind Annenberg, Award Winning Addiction Educator, Los Angeles, CA

Religion

Men never do evil so completely and cheerfully as when they do it from religious conviction.

- Blaise Pascal, French Mathematician, Inventor, and Philosopher, 1623-1662

Religion and Politics

In religion and politics, people's beliefs and convictions are, in almost every case, gotten secondhand and without examination.

- Mark Twain, American Author, 1835-1910

Religions For Peace?

There is an idea that religions usher peace into the world. Unfortunately, that idea doesn't really hold up historically.

- Jerry Tigre, Australian Author of *"Religions of Peace?"*, 1907-1962

Religious Originality

I'm a religious original.

- Abraham Lincoln, 16th President of the United States, 1809-1865

Remedies Can Hurt Too

Some remedies are worse than the disease.

- Publilius Syrus, Syrian Author and Philosopher, 85-43 BCE

Reputation

If you hurt the reputation of another, you damage your own.

- Hawaiian Saying

Respect Children

The commandment tells us that we must honor our mother and father. I have another commandment that is just as important.

Commandment 5 ½. "In all ways and every day, Honor Your Children."

- Larry Chroman, Extraordinary Special Education Teacher, 1951-2021

Respect Joke

My daughter thinks I don't respect her personal boundaries. Or at least that's what she wrote in her diary.

- Sonia Little, LLanybydder Community Primary School Parent, Carmarthenshire, Wales, U.K. 2004

Respect Towards You

When you are content to be simply yourself and don't compare or compete, everybody will respect you.

- Lao Tzu, Legendary Chinese Philosopher, 604-531 BCE

Respect Yourself

If you want to be respected, you must respect yourself.

- Spanish Prover

Respecting Kids

I like children. I like 'em, and I respect 'em. Pretty much all the honest truth-telling there is in the world is done by them.

- Oliver Wendell Holmes Jr., American Judge, 1841-1935

Responsibility and Authority

It is the first responsibility of every citizen to question authority.

- Ben Franklin, American Inventor, Printer, and Political Philosopher, 1706-1790

Responsibility and Power

With great power comes great responsibility.

- Voltaire, French Author and Playwright, 1693-1778. (Spiderman also says this)

Responsibility Towards Our Youth

Let us put our minds together and see what life we can make for our children.

- Sitting Bull, Lakota Chief, 1831-1890

Responsible For Ourselves

We each decide whether to make ourselves learned or ignorant, compassionate or cruel, generous or miserly. No one forces us. No one decides for us. No one drags us along one path or the other. We are responsible for what we are.

- Maimonides, Spanish/Egyptian Talmudist, physician, Philosopher, 1138-1204

Results

Don't tell people what you plan to do. Show them what you've completed.

- Ivan Abgari Adamian, Armenian Engineer, 1879-1932

Revenge

The man who seeks revenge digs two graves.

- Ken Kesey, American Novelist, 1935-2001

Revolution Takes Time

Creating a revolution in South America is like plowing the ocean.

- Simon Bolivar, Liberator of most of South America from Spain, 1783-1830

Revolution is a Right

When dictatorship is a fact, revolution becomes a right.

- Victor Hugo, French Author,1802-1885

Revolution or Not

Before you destroy something, better make sure you have something good to replace it.

- Miguel de Cervantes, Spanish Author, 1547-1616

Revolution: Peaceful or Violent

Those who make peaceful revolution impossible will make violent revolution inevitable.

- John F Kennedy, 35th President of the United States, 1917-1963

Right and Wrong

Even a broken clock is right twice a day. After a few years it can even boast of a long series of successes.

- Marie Von Ebner-Eschenbach, Austrian Author, 1830-1916

Risk

A turtle travels only when it sticks its neck out.

- Korean Proverb

Rites of Passage

Rite of passage refers to an event that helps you achieve a new sense of confidence, and a new, expanded sense of self.

- Ellen Chroman, Master Gardener, 1955-2020

Rites of Passage 2

Throughout time and all over the planet, cultures have created rituals and ceremonies that honor and support a young person's transition from childhood to maturity. These are frequently called Rites of Passage. The participant engages in a difficult test in order to prove to themselves and to the community that they are worthy of entering this new, valued position within the culture.

- Alice Cunningham Fletcher, American Ethnologist and Anthropologist 1862-1921

Romance Joke

I like to hold hands at the movies... which always seems to startle strangers.

- Richie's Great Big Chicago Joke Book

Roman Numeral Joke

A Roman soldier walks into a restaurant, holds up two fingers, and says, "Table for five, please."

- Richie's Great Big Chicago Joke Book

Romantic Alphabet

If I could rearrange the alphabet,
I'd put U and I together.

- Ann Onymous,

Official Feet Warmer for Louise, Duchess of Fife, 1867-1931

Romantic Compliment

Your eyes are the brightest stars I have ever seen.

- Leonard Von Sacher-Masoch, Austrian Novelist, 1836-1895

Romantic Kiss

Kissing is the language of love, so let us begin our conversation.

- Ann Onymous, Official Feet Warmer for Louise, Duchess of Fife, 1867-1931

Romantic Point

Life without knowing you would be like a broken pencil, pointless.

- Ann Onymous, Official Feet Warmer for Louise, Duchess of Fife, 1867-1931

Royalty Joke

Q. Why did the queen go to the dentist?

A. To get crowns on her teeth.

- Richie's Great Big Chicago Joke Book

Rules for Fools

1. *Find the fullness in the broken.*

2. *Find the extraordinary in the ordinary.*

3. *As long as you are walking on thin ice, you might as well dance.*

- Paddy O'Furniture, Irish Clown, 1890-1930

S

Sadness & Joy

The deeper that sorrow carves into your being, the more joy you can contain.

- Kahlil Gibran, Lebanese-American Author and poet, 1883-1931

Sadness & Knowledge

When your knowledge increases, so does your sorrow.

- Romanian Proverb

Sadness Created

One moment's error becomes a lifetime of sadness.

- Chinese Proverb

Safe from Harm

Before you taunt a cobra, make sure your stick is long.

- Egyptian Proverb

Sanctuary in Yourself

Make it a priority to look, because inside of you there is a stillness and a sanctuary where you can relax. But.......you have look until you find it.

- Altaf Hussain Hali, Urdu Poet, 1837-1913

Scars
He who laughs at a scar never felt a wound.

- German Proverb

School and a Mother's Heart

A mother's heart is the most important school.

School Has Its Limits

A child educated only at school is an uneducated child.

- George Santayana, Spanish-American Philosopher and Novelist, 1863-1952

School and in the Kitchen

A foreign language is more easily learned in the kitchen than at school.

- Ukrainian Proverb

School Joke

Q. *Did you hear about the kid who bungee jumped from the school's flagpole?*

A. *He was suspended.*

- Richie's Great Big Chicago Joke Book

School Joke 2

Q. *What did the janitor say when he jumped out of the closet?*

A. *"Supplies!"*

- Richie's Great Big Chicago Joke Book

Schools Close Prisons

He who opens a school door, closes a prison.

- Victor Hugo, French Author,1802-1855

Schools & Teachers

Most naughtiness arises because children are bored and because of lack of a positive relationship with the teacher.

- Rudolph Steiner, Austrian Educator and Architect, 1861-1925

Scientific Prediction in 1923

It will soon be possible to transmit wireless messages around the world so simply that any individual can carry and operate his own apparatus.

- Nikola Tesla, Austrian/American Inventor and Futurist, 1856-1943

Secret Lives

Every person lives his real, most interesting life under the cover of secrecy.

- Anton Chekhov, Russian Author, 1860-1904

Seeking and Finding

Seek patiently, you will find.

- Found in the Egyptian Temple of Luxor

Self-Acceptance

This above all: To thine own self be true.

- William Shakespeare, English Playwright, 1564-1616

Self-Affirming

I prefer to be true to myself, even at the hazard of incurring the ridicule of others.

- Frederick Douglass, African American Social Reformer, Statesman, 1818-1895

Self-Assured

One who believes in himself has no need to convince others.

- Lao Tzu, Legendary Chinese Philosopher, 604-531 BCE

Self-Knowledge

Know thyself.

- Socrates, Greek Philosopher, 469-399 BCE

Self-Respect

Respect yourself, and others will respect you.

- Confucius, Chinese Philosopher, 551 - 479 BCE

Self-Responsibility

If you could kick the person in the pants who is responsible for most of your trouble, you wouldn't sit for a month.

- Theodore Roosevelt, 26th President, 1858-1919

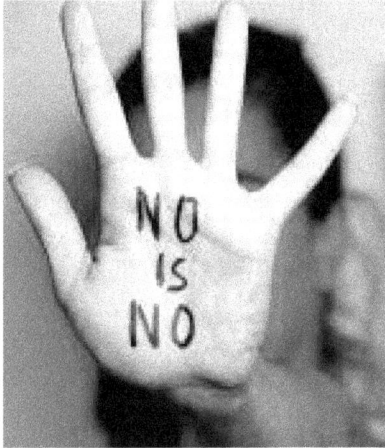

Sexual Boundary Language

Saying "no" can be very tough sometimes, but it is important to remember that it is your right to do so. It's helpful to have a few different ways of saying "no" in your toolbox, whether it's a gentle but firm statement or a nonverbal cue like moving away. It's important to communicate your boundaries clearly and effectively. Doing nothing doesn't send a clear message and can actually be confusing for the other person.

- Lotus Ramsey, Author of The Lotus Report, 2004

Sex and Emotions

Sex is deeply emotional. It's not just a physical act. Teens need to remember this when they get involved.

- Lotus Ramsey, Author of The Lotus Report, 2004

Sex and Trust

You need to really trust the other person. You need to know that they care about you. You need to feel a sense of freedom, attraction, and humor with them. Most of all, you need to be able to relax with your partner.

- Lotus Ramsey, Author of The Lotus Report, 2004

Sexual Safety

It may be embarrassing to talk about, but we need to have that conversation about

.......Condoms. People have been using condoms, in one form or another, since the 1400's. A quality condom works well to block the spread of sexually transmitted diseases and to reduce the risk of pregnancy. Anyone can walk into a drug store and buy them. There is no age requirement, and no prescription is necessary. Take responsibility for yourself and your partner. If you are going to have sex, use a condom.

- Lotus Ramsey, Author of The Lotus Report, 2004

Sexual Safety Jingle

If you can't shield your rocket, leave it in your pocket.

- Cliff Hanger, Canadian Stand-up Comedian, 1930-1974

Shakespeare's Best Insults

You mad, mustached, purple-hued malt worm.

- William Shakespeare, English Playwright 1564-1616

Shakespeare's Best Insults 2

More of your conversation would infect my brain.

- William Shakespeare, English Playwright 1564-1616

Shakespeare's Best Insults 3

You have no more brains than I have in my elbows.

- William Shakespeare, English Playwright 1564-1616

Short People

My grandfather was so small he could dance in between the toes of a baby.

- Penny Whistle, My cousin's grandma's neighbor in Omaha Nebraska.

Short People 2

Things smell different to short people, especially in elevators.

- Will Rogers, American Humorist, 1879-1935

Sibling Gifts

The greatest gift our parents ever gave us was each other.

- Thea Chroman, Working Mom and eldest of my 12 daughters.

Sickness and Health

During sickness, you recognize the value of good health.

- Sicilian Proverb

Sickness, Coming and Going

Sickness charges in on horseback but departs limping on foot.

- Dutch Proverb

Sight Joke

Q. Why did the man fall down the well?

A. He couldn't see that well.

- Richie's Great Big Chicago Joke Book

Silence Speaks Loudly

Sometimes you have to be silent to be heard.

- Swiss Proverb

Silence Your Mind

Learn to be silent. Let your quiet mind listen and absorb.

- Pythagoras, Greek Philosopher, 570-490 BCE

Simplicity

Simplicity is the final achievement.

- Frederic Chopin, Polish Composer and Pianist, 1810-1849

Simplify

Too many generals can ruin an army.

- Homer, Greek Poet, 8th Century BCE

Sing, Love, and Dance

Go out in the world and ... sing as if no one is listening, love as if you have never been hurt, and dance as if no one is watching.

- Victor Hugo, French Author,1802-1885

Sleep

A clear conscience is the best pillow.

- American Proverb

Slow Growing

The finest timbers come from the slowest-growing trees.

- American Proverb

Small Towns Can Be Mean

God made nature.
Man made the city.
But the devil made the small town.

- American Saying

Smart?

If you are the smartest person in the room, then you are in the wrong room.

- Confucius, Chinese Philosopher, 551 - 479 BCE

Smelling a Foreign County

The first condition of understanding a foreign country is to smell it.

- Rudyard Kipling, English Author and Poet, 1865-1936

Smoking & Love

You can't smoke and love yourself at the same time.

- Ashley Delaune, Yucatan Jungle Guide

Smoking Cigarettes

Quitting cigarettes is easy. I've done it at least 50 times.

- Mark Twain, American Author, 1835-1910

Social Media

The "like" button and the use of artificial intelligence to promote excessive scrolling may be dangerous for developing brains.

- American Psychiatric Association

Social Media Addiction

If you find yourself choosing to be on social media most of the time, then you really need to consider a detox.

- Ira Williams, Television Personality, Galway Ireland

Soil and the Future

Fertility of the soil is the future of civilization.

- Albert Howard, English Botanist, 1873-1947

Soil and the Foundation Nations

A nation that destroys its soil destroys itself.

- Ben Franklin, Inventor, Printer, and Political Philosopher, 1706-1790

Soil with Artificial Nutrients

Chemically soaked soil and artificial manures inevitably lead to artificial nutrition, artificial food, artificial animals, and finally, artificial men and women.

- Albert Howard, English Botanist, 1873-1947

Solitude

The fool needs constant company. The wise need frequent solitude.

- Jewish Proverb

Solitude and Genius

Solitude is the school of genius.

- Edward Gibbon, English Essayist, Historian, and Politician. 1737-1794

Solitude as Company

I love to be alone. I never found a companion that was so companionable as solitude.

- Henry David Thoreau, American Philosopher, 1817-1862

Solitude: Beneficial or Harmful

Solitude either develops the mental powers or renders men dull and vicious.

- Victor Hugo, French Author,1802-1885

Sorrow and Friends

Sorrows are hidden treasures that you only show to your friends.

- Spanish Proverb

Space Alien Joke

Q. Why don't space aliens like to eat clowns?

A. Because they taste funny!

- Richie's Great Big Chicago Joke Book

Speaking at the Right Time

Remember not only to say the right thing in the right place but, far more difficult still, to leave unsaid the wrong thing at the tempting moment.

- Ben Franklin, Inventor, Printer, and Political Philosopher, 1706-1790

Speaking Freely

In a free state, there should be freedom of speech and thought.

- Tiberius, Roman Emperor, 43 BCE- 37 CE

Speaking Freely Is a Right

I disapprove of what you say but will defend to the death your right to say it.

- Voltaire, French Author and Philosopher, 1694-1778

Speaking Mean of Others

The tongue is soft, but it cuts deep.

- Spanish Saying

Speaking (or Not)

When I think over what I have said, I envy the mute.

- Seneca the Younger, Roman Philosopher, 4 BCE- 65 CE

Speaking Truth

Speak the truth, but leave immediately after.

- Slovenian Proverb

Speaking with Anger

Speak when you are angry, and you will make the best speech you will ever regret.

Ambrose Bierce, American Author, 1842-1914

Speaking with Restraint

If you have guarded your mouth from thoughtless speech, your days will be peaceful.

- Talmud

Sports and Health

Sports help preserve health.

- Hippocrates, Greek Physician, 460-370 BCE

Stars Beyond Measure

Scientists agree that there are about 400 billion stars in our galaxy.

They tell us that there are roughly a billion galaxies.

That means that if there is roughly the same amount of stars in each galaxy, then there are around 1,000,000,000,000,000,000,000,000 stars out there. (Not to mention the planets.)

- Justin Idea, Griffith Park Observatory Presenter, Los Angeles CA, 1968

Start, Don't Just Stand There!

You can't cross the sea merely by standing and staring at the water..

- Rabindranath Tagore, Indian Playwright and Poet, 1861-1941

Start Weaving Your Life

Begin to weave, and God will give the thread.

- Guatemalan Proverb

Starting Now

The secret to getting ahead is getting started.

- Mark Twain, American Author, 1835-1910

Starting takes Courage

Courage is the commitment to begin without any guarantee of success.

- Johann Wolfgang von Goethe, German Author, 1749-1832

Stillness

The inspiration you seek is already within you. Be still and listen.

- Rumi, Islamic Poet and Mystic, 1207-1273

Stillness and Secrets

Be still. Stillness reveals the secrets of eternity.

- Lao Tzu, Legendary Chinese Philosopher, 604-531 BCE

Stories and Our Uniqueness

God made people because he loves stories.

- Yiddish Proverb

Stories and Therapy

Some people go to therapy. Some people go to church or temple. Some of us go to stories.

- Noah Zark, Storyteller at the Renaissance Faire, Agoura CA. 1973

Stories To Einstein

If you want your child to be intelligent, read them fairy tales. If you want them to be more intelligent, read them more fairy tales.

- Albert Einstein, German-born Theoretical Physicist, 1879-1955

Storytelling

I never lie. Telling the truth is too much fun.

- April Foolz, 95 year old Professional Boxer and Contortionist.

Strength and Power

Mastering others is strength. Mastering yourself is true power.

- Lao Tzu, Legendary Chinese Philosopher, 604-531 BCE

Strength and Slow Progress

I am a slow walker, but I never walk back.

- Abraham Lincoln, 16th President of the United States, 1809-1865

Struggle is Important

It is only by struggling courageously against overwhelming odds that man can succeed in wringing meaning out of his existence.

- Sigmund Freud, Austrian Founder of Psychoanalysis, 1856-1939

Stupidity Hurts

Stupidity is a disease without a medicine.

- Arabic Proverb

Stupid Plus Aggressive

There is nothing worse than aggressive stupidity.

- Johann Wolfgang von Goethe, German Author, 1749-1832

Succeed with Boldness

Success is the child of boldness.

- Benjamin Disraeli, British statesman and Politician, 1804-1881

Success

I'm a success today because I had a friend who believed in me, and I didn't have the heart to let him down.

- Abraham Lincoln, 16th President of the United States, 1809-1865

Success and Determination

Success waits patiently for anyone who has the determination and strength to seize it.

- Booker T. Washington, Civil Rights Activist and Educator, 1856-1915

Switzerland Joke

Q. What's the best thing   about Switzerland?

A. Well, to start with, their flag is a big plus.

- Richie's Great Big Chicago Joke Book

T

Tact, Not Enemies

Tact is the art of making a point without making an enemy.

- Isaac Newton, English Mathematician, Physicist, Astronomer, 1643-172

Talking

After all is said and done, more is said than done.

- Aesop, Greek Slave and Storyteller, 620-556 BCE

Talking and Talkers

People who know little are usually great talkers, while men who know much say little.

- Jean Jacques Rousseau, Swiss-French Philosopher, 1712-1778

Talking and Thinking

The less men think, the more they talk.

- Montesquieu, French Philosopher,1689-1755

Talking Joke

I accidentally handed my wife a glue stick instead of a Chapstick. She still isn't talking to me.

- Richie's Great Big Chicago Joke Book

Talking with Care

Letting the cat out of the bag is a whole lot easier than putting it back in.

- Anton Chekhov, Russian Author, 1860-1904

Taste

My tastes are simple: I am easily satisfied with the best.

- Anton Chekhov, Russian Author, 1860-1904

Teacher Joke

Q. Why did they fire the cross-eyed teacher?

A. She couldn't control her pupils.

- Richie's Great Big Chicago Joke Book

Teachers Appear

When a student is ready, a teacher appears.

- Lao Tzu, Legendary Chinese Philosopher, 604-531 BCE

Teaching By Encouragement

Correction does much, but encouragement does more.

- Johann Wolfgang von Goethe, German Author, 1749-1832

Teaching Others

By teaching others, you will learn yourself.

- George Gurdjieff, Armenian/Greek Philosopher and Mystic, 1866-1949

Teaching Simplicity

You don't have to say anything. You don't have to teach anything. You just have to be who you are: a bright flame shining in the darkness of despair, a shining example of a person able to cross bridges by opening your heart and mind.

- Tsoknyi Rinpoche, Tibetan Buddhist Teacher and Author, 1964-

Teenagers are Remarkable

I love working with Teenagers. They are engagingly alive, wonderfully honest, amazingly curious, remarkably fun, and frequently extremely serious about life, now and into the future.

- Izzi Tooinsky, King of Hotdogastan, 1929

Teenagers Meat Joke

Q. Why do teenagers love meat so much?

A. Because meat is always protein.

- Richie's Great Big Chicago Joke Book

Teenagers in Antiquity

Teenagers these days are out of control. They eat like pigs, they are disrespectful to adults, they interrupt and contradict their parents, and they terrorize their teachers.

- Aristotle, Greek Philosopher, 384-322 BCE

Teenagers in Antiquity 2

They disrespect their elders; they disobey their parents. They ignore the law. They riot in the streets, inflamed with wild notions.

- Plato, Greek Philosopher, 424-348 BCE

Temptation

I can resist anything except temptation.

- Oscar Wilde, Irish Playwright and Poet, 1854-1900

Tenacity to Rise

Fall seven times, stand up eight.

- Japanese Proverb

Tenacity Until Death

I would rather die on my feet than live on my knees.

- Euripides, Greek Playwright, 485-403 BCE

Terror, Felt by All

Teenagers listen! The fears, doubts, anxieties, and terrors that you feel in your own heart are not just yours. These are felt by humans across time and place. It is human to feel these. It's also human to heal from these.

- Izzi Tooinsky, King of Hotdogastan, 1929-

Terror of the Brave

Even the bravest of men experience sudden terror.

- Tacitus, Roman Historian and Politician, 55 BCE -120

Think for Yourself

To find yourself, think for yourself.

- Socrates, Greek Philosopher 469-399 BCE

Thinking Should Shape Opinion

Too often, we enjoy the comfort of opinion without the discomfort of thought.

- John F Kennedy, 35th President of the United States, 1917-1963

Thinking or Rearranging

A great many people think they are thinking when they are merely rearranging their prejudices.

- William James, American Philosopher, 1842-1910

Training Matters

He who sweats more in training bleeds less in war.

- Spartan Saying

Trap Riddle

Don't spell part backwards. It's a trap.

- Richie's Great Big Chicago Joke Book

Trauma & Healing

Your trauma is not your fault, but healing is your responsibility.

- Paulette Mahurin, My Cousin and well-known author of *The Seven Year Dress* and many other novels.

Travel Addiction

Travel is the healthiest addiction.

- Steve Clements, My Old Buddy From Hotdogastan

Travel Joke

Q. What travels the world but stays in one corner?

A. A stamp

- Richie's Great Big Chicago Joke Book

Travel Magic

Travel brings excitement and love back into your life.

- Rumi, Islamic Poet and Mystic,

1207-1273

Travel To Find Yourself

A wise man travels to discover himself.

- James Russell Lowell, American poet., 1819-189

Travel Therapy

I wish travel therapy was covered by my health insurance.

- A guy at the bus station in Tulum Mexico said this to me in 1973

Traveler's Advice

A good traveler has no fixed plans and is not intent on arriving on a certain date.

- Lao Tzu, Legendary Chinese Philosopher, 604-531 BCE

Traveler's Humility

Travel makes one modest. You see what a tiny place you occupy in the world.

- Gustave Flaubert, French Novelist, 1821-1880

Traveler's Truth

I've been a traveler most all of my life. When I'm wandering, I'm constantly reminded of the generosity of the poor and the good humor of children.

- Bharatchandra Roy, Indian Poet, 1712-1760

Traveling Light Joke

A photon was going through airport security. The TSA agent asked if she had any luggage. The photon answered, "No, I'm traveling light.

- Richie's Great Big Chicago Joke Book

Treasures of Lao Tzu

I have just three things to teach:
Simplicity, Patience, and Compassion.
These three are the greatest treasures.

- Lao Tzu, Legendary Chinese Philosopher,
604-531 BCE

Tree Joke

Q. How can you tell a tree is a dogwood tree?

A. By its bark.

- Richie's Great Big Chicago Joke Book

Triangle Joke

Q. What did the circle say to the triangle?

A. I see your point.

- Richie's Great Big Chicago Joke Book

Trickster & Laughter

If you want to tell people the truth, make them laugh. Otherwise, they'll kill you.

- George Bernard Shaw, Irish Playwright, 1856-1950

Trickster & Laughter 2

Often, truth will only be tolerated when it's dressed up like folly.

- Bharatchandra Roy, Indian Poet, 1712-1760

Trust

Be careful who you trust. Even the devil was once an angel.

- Turkish Proverb

Truth and Falsehood

All that glitters is not gold.

- William Shakespeare, English Playwright 1564-1616

Truth is Simple

It does not require many words to speak the truth.

- Chief Joseph, Nez Perce Leader, 1849-1904

Truth Rises

Truth and oil always come to the surface.

- Spanish Proverb

Truth Slap

Better to be slapped with the truth than to be kissed by a lie.

- Russian Proverb

Truth Speaks

No man is hated more than he who speaks the truth.

- Plato, Greek Philosopher, 447-327 BCE

Truth Telling

A jest is half a truth.

- Persian Proverb

Truth Will Not be Drowned

You will not drown the truth in seas of blood.

- Maxim Gorky, Russian Author, 1868-1936

Tyrants and Power

Those who voluntarily put power into the hands of a tyrant must not wonder if it is at last turned against themselves.

- Aesop, Greek Slave and Storyteller, 620-556 BCE

Tyrants Fall

When I despair, I remember that all through history, the way of truth and love have always won. There have been tyrants and murderers, and for a time, they can seem invincible, but in the end, they always fall. Think of it – always.

- Mahatma Gandhi, Nonviolent Anti Colonialist, Politician, 1869-1948

U

Understanding the Universe

I didn't arrive at my understanding of the fundamental laws of the universe through my rational mind.

- Albert Einstein, German-born Theoretical Physicist, 1879-1955

Unhappiness

Much unhappiness has come from things left unsaid.

- Leo Tolstoy, Russian Author, 1828-1910

Unhappiness and Wealth

Man's obsession to add to his wealth and honor is the chief source of his misery.

- Maimonides, Spanish/Egyptian Talmudist, physician, Philosopher, 1138-1204

Unhappy Snail

She was as unhappy as a snail on a waffle iron.

- American Saying

Universal Understanding

Everyone who is seriously involved in the pursuit of science becomes convinced that some spirit is manifest in the laws of the universe, one that is vastly superior to that of man.

- Albert Einstein, German-born Theoretical Physicist, 1879-1955

Universe

The word universe means "One Song."

- Aarav Aditi, Indian Teacher of Astronomy, 1893-1963

Unwelcomed

He is as unwelcome as a rattlesnake at a garden party.

- American Expression

V

Value

No one is useless in this world who lightens the burden of it to anyone else.

- Charles Dickens, English Author, 1812-1870

Vegetable Joke

Q: What do you call an everyday potato?

A: A commentator.

- Richie's Great Big Chicago Joke Book

Vegetarian Hunter Joke

"Vegetarian" is an old Celtic word for "a really bad hunter."

- Richie's Great Big Chicago Joke Book

Vegetarian Joke

Being a vegetarian is a big, missed steak.

- Graffiti I saw at the 12th Annual Texas Steak Cookoff, Hico Texas

Vegetarian Question

Can a vegetarian eat
animal crackers?

- Little boy's question at my
  performance in Auckland
  New Zealand

  2007

Vegetarianism

Animals are my friends, and I don't eat my friends.

- George Bernard Shaw, Irish Playwright, 1856-1950

Violence Joke

Q. Waiter: "Do you wanna box for your leftovers?"

A. Mike: "No, but I'll wrestle you for the dessert."

- Richie's Great Big Chicago Joke Book

Violence Joke 2

Two peanuts were walking down the street in a bad part of town. One peanut was not hurt, but the other was a salted.

- Richie's Great Big Chicago Joke Book

Vision and Yearning

If you want to build a ship, don't drum up men together to gather wood, divide the work, and give orders. Instead, teach them to yearn for the vast and endless sea.

- Antoine De Saint-Exupery, French Author, and Pioneering Aviator, 1900-1944

Vision Takes Work

The man who moves a mountain begins by carrying away small stones.

- Confucius, Chinese Philosopher, 551-479 BCE

W

Wages

*If you pay peanuts, you
get monkeys.*

- English Parable

Waiting Joke

Q. Why did the little cookie cry?

A. Because his dad was a wafer so long.

- Richie's Great Big Chicago Joke Book

Walk with Nature

In every walk with nature, one receives far more than he seeks.

- John Muir, Father of the American National Parks, 1838-1914

Walking & Thinking

All truly great thoughts are conceived while walking.

- Fredrich Nietzsche, German Philosopher, 1844-1900

Walking at Night

Although I am an old man, night is generally my time for walking.

- Charles Dickens, English Author, 1812-1870

Walking is Medicine

Walking is man's best medicine.

- Hippocrates, Greek Physician, 460-370 BCE

Walking With Thomas Jefferson

The object of walking is to relax the mind. It is the best possible exercise. There is no habit you will value so much as that of walking far.

- Thomas Jefferson, 3rd President of the United States, 1743-1826

Wandering is Valuable

He who wanders finds new paths.

- Norwegian Proverb

War and Peace

In peace, sons bury their fathers. In war, fathers bury their sons.

- Herodotus, Greek Historian, 484-425 BCE

War Casualties

In a battle between elephants, it's the ants that get squashed.

- Thai Proverb

War Joke

War is God's way of teaching Americans geography.

- Ambrose Bierce, American Author, 1842-1914

War Joke 2

Q. Where does the king of Denmark keep his armies?

A. In his sleevies.

- Richie's Great Big Chicago Joke Book

War Thinking

It is more important to out-think your enemy than to out-fight him.

- Sun Tzu, Chinese Military General, 545-496 BCE

Warrior's Purpose

I am a warrior, so that my son may be a merchant, so that his son may be a poet.

- John Quincy Adams, 6th President of U.S.A, 1767-1848

Warriors: Time and Patience

The strongest of all warriors are these two — Time and Patience.

- Leo Tolstoy, Russian Author, 1828-1910

Waste of Time

If you only row with one oar, you go in a circle.

- Athabascan Proverb

Weakness

The weak can never forgive. Forgiveness is the attribute of the strong.

- Mahatma Gandhi, Nonviolent Anti Colonialist, Politician, 1869-1948

Wealth and Contentment

He is the richest who is content with the least.

- Socrates, Greek Philosopher, 469-399 BCE

Wealth and Greed

Great wealth generally makes great greed.

- French Proverb

Wealth & Heaven

It is easier for a camel to go through the eye of a needle than for a rich man to enter the kingdom of heaven.

- Jesus of Nazareth, Religious Leader, 4 BCE-33

Wealth for the Rich

The comfort of the rich depends upon an abundant supply of the poor.

- Voltaire, French Author and Philosopher, 1694-1778

Weather & Clothes

There is no such thing as bad weather, only bad clothing choices.

- Scandinavian Saying

Weather Joke

Q. What's a tornado's favorite game to play?

A. Twister!

- Richie's Great Big Chicago Joke Book

What Matters

All that matters is what we do for each other.

- Lewis Carroll, English Author, 1832-1898

Wilderness for Rest

Come to the woods, for here is rest.

- John Muir, Father of the American National Parks, 1838-1914

Will Joke

Where there's a will, there's a relative.

- Will Rogers, American Humorist, 1879-1935

Will or Wish

The most important thing in life is to stop saying 'I wish' and start saying, 'I will.' Consider nothing impossible, then treat possibilities as probabilities.

- Charles Dickens, English Author, 1812-1870

Will vs Strength

People do not lack strength; they lack will.

- Victor Hugo, French Author,1802-1885

Wisdom and Experience

Good judgment comes from experience, and experience comes from bad judgment.

- Will Rogers, American Humorist, 1879-1935

Wisdom and Foolishness

The fool thinks he is wise, but the wise man knows himself to be a fool.

- William Shakespeare, English Playwright 1564-1616

Wisdom & Knowledge

Knowledge is not necessarily wisdom.

- Found in the Egyptian Temple of Luxor

Wisdom's Cheer

The most certain sign of wisdom is cheerfulness.

- Michel de Montaigne, French Philosopher, 1513-1592

Wisdom's Humility

The more wisdom you acquire, the humbler you become.

- Armenian Saying

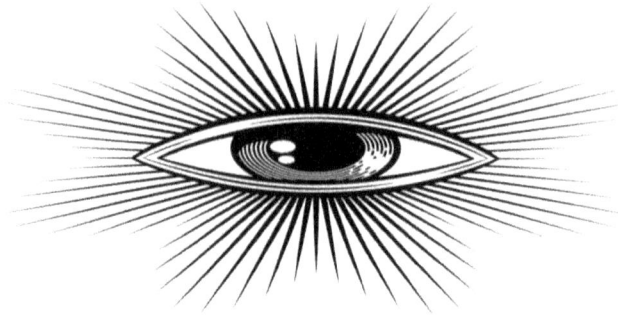

Wisdom's Realization

True wisdom comes to each of us when we realize how little we understand about life, ourselves, and the world around us.

- Socrates, Greek Philosopher, 469-399 BCE

Wisdom's View

The invariable mark of wisdom is to see the miraculous in the common.

- Ralph Waldo Emerson, American Philosopher, 1803-1882

Woman

And

Civilization

Women...in the future will startle civilization with their progress.

- *Nikola Tesla, Austrian/American Inventor and Futurist*

1856-1943

Women and the Impossible

Women, like men, should try to do the impossible.

- Amelia Earhart, American Aviation Pioneer and Author, 1897-1937

Wonder To Wonder

Existence opens from wonder to wonder.

- Lao Tzu, Legendary Chinese Philosopher, 604-531 BCE

Wonders Can Grow

Marvelous wonders don't have to happen all of a sudden, the way they do in the Arabian Nights. They can also take a long time, like crystals growing, or minds changing, or leaves turning. The trick is to keep an eye peeled, so they don't slip by unappreciated.

- Ken Kesey, American Novelist, 1935-2001

Words Fly Like Spears

Words are like spears. Once they leave your lips they can never come back.

- Malawian Proverb

Word Joke

Thanks for explaining the word "sundry" to me; it means a lot.

- Richie's Great Big Chicago Joke Book

Words Make a House

The words you speak become the house you live in.

- Hafez, Persian Poet, 1325-1390

Work

A bad worker blames his tools.

- Australian Proverb

Work and Love

Work is love made visible.

- Kahlil Gibran, Lebanese American Author and poet, 1883-1931

Work, Close at Hand

If you need a helping hand, you'll find one at the end of your arm.

- Persian Proverb

Work Joke

I can't believe I got fired from the calendar factor; all I did was take a day off!

- Richie's Great Big Chicago Joke Book

Work Joke 2

Q. Why did they fire the lady from the orange juice factory?

A. She couldn't concentrate.

- Richie's Great Big Chicago Joke Book

Work Made Easy

Many hands make light work.

- Russian Proverb

Work Now

Make hay while the sun shines.

- English Proverb

Work: Thunder and Lightning

It's better to have less thunder in the mouth and more lightning in the hand.

- Apache Saying

Worry's Shadow

Worry gives a small thing a big shadow.

- Swedish Proverb

Wrong Joke

Q. What word is always spelled wrong?

A. Wrong

- Richie's Great Big Chicago Joke Book

Wrong By Many

Wrong does not cease to be wrong because the majority share in it.

- Leo Tolstoy, Russian Author, 1828-1910

Y

Young and Old

To be seventy years young is sometimes far more cheerful and hopeful than to be forty years old.

- Oliver Wendell Holmes Jr., American Judge, 1841-1935

Yourself

Be yourself. There's nothing more Bad Ass than that!

- Pearl Merriweather, High School P.E. Teacher in Perth Australia

Yourself is Available

Be yourself; everyone else is already taken.

- Oscar Wilde, Irish Playwright and Poet, 1854-1900

Youth

Youth is quick in feeling but weak in judgment.

- Homer, Greek Poet, 800-850 BCE

Youth and Age

Youth is wasted on the young.

- George Bernard Shaw, Irish Playwright, 1856-1950

Youth and Knowledge

I'm not young enough to know everything.

- Oscar Wilde, Irish Playwright and Poet, 1854-1900

Youth and Old Age

In youth, we learn; in old age we understand.

- Ecuadorian Saying

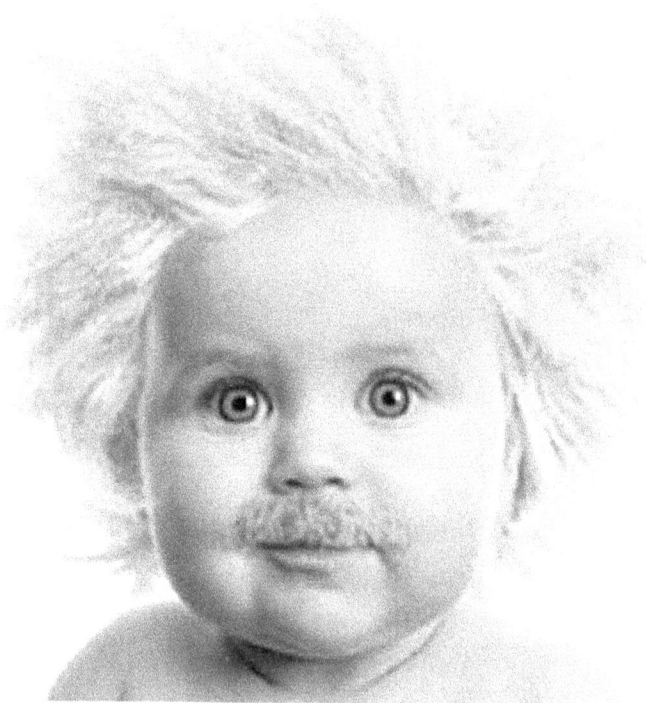

Z

Zeal

Zeal without knowledge is a runaway horse.

- German Proverb

Zealous Parents

Too many parents make life hard for their children by trying, too zealously, to make it easy for them.

- Johann Wolfgang von Goethe, German Author, 1749-1832

Zest

Zest is what makes life sparkle.

It's the love in the love letter.

It's the heart in the heart-throb.

It's the fun in the funky.

It's the pow in the pow-wow.

It's the yip in the yippie yeah.

To find your way, find your Zest.

- Izzi Tooinsky, King of Hotdogastan, 1929-

You Count!

Well my dears, you have finished reading, but you haven't completed the book, because this book cannot be completed. It is always changing, and you are part of that change. Now, pay attention, because the time has come for you to participate in the ongoing life of this ancient manuscript.

Here's what you need to do: As you go along your days and nights, whether you are alone, with friends or family, at school, in the woods, or 1000 other possibilities, keep your eyes and ears open.

Watch and listen for the jewels of insight, for the preciousness of true wisdom, and for the sparkling nuggets of great jokes. Catch them, before they are swept away by the winds of time. Write them in your 10 pages. And please send them to me at teencompass1@gmail.com.

Remember, the gems that you collect now will be included in future versions of this book. Your quotes will be gifts for those young people who will come after you. The sayings, jokes and proverbs you collect now will help those kids of the future to be stronger, happier, and smarter inhabitants of this wonderful planet.

And as for me, Izzi Tooinsky, the King of Hotdogastan, I want to leave you with one last quote concerning your lives and the lives of future Teenagers. It was written by my dear friend Walt Whitman. It's a good one to memorize.

"The strangest and sweetest songs yet remain to be sung."

My Proverbs, Quotes, Sayings, and Jokes

My Proverbs, Quotes, Sayings, and Jokes

A TEENAGER'S COMPASS TO LIFE

Funny, wise, inspirational, and transformational, this book relays the wit and wisdom of many of the greatest thinkers, leaders, and fools ever to walk this earth. With equal measures of jokes, quotes, and proverbs, A Teenager's Compass To Life skillfully points our young people in the direction of authenticity, bravery, loyalty, resilience, and most importantly, being true to oneself.

Izzi Tooinsky, award-winning juggler, storyteller, and the King of Hotdogastan, shares with us this ancient, ever-changing book. While the entries are only a line or two, each is filled with the proverbial wisdom of the ages (and a few jokes). Perfect for today's teenagers.

ISBN 9798991454728

90000

9 798991 454728

My Proverbs, Quotes, Sayings, and Jokes

My Proverbs, Quotes, Sayings, and Jokes

My Proverbs, Quotes, Sayings, and Jokes

My Proverbs, Quotes, Sayings, and Jokes

My Proverbs, Quotes, Sayings, and Jokes

My Proverbs, Quotes, Sayings, and Jokes

My Proverbs, Quotes, Sayings, and Jokes

My Proverbs, Quotes, Sayings, and Jokes

About the Author

Izzi Tooinsky, an award-winning Juggler and Storyteller, is the King of Hotdogastan. Half the year, he travels the world performing Juggling/Comedy shows in order to raise funds for his royal treasury. The other half of the year he lives in Hotdogastan, taking care of his people through stories, jokes, proverbs, and of course, through the joy of juggling.

www.ingramcontent.com/pod-product-compliance
Lightning Source LLC
Chambersburg PA
CBHW081147270326
41930CB00014B/3070